About the author

Wilfred Emmanuel-Jones is, in his own words, 'a poor boy, done good'. He was born in Frankfield, Clarendon, Jamaica and then, after his parents moved to the UK in the fifties, was raised in inner-city Birmingham.

Having proved a challenging school student, in part due to unacknowledged dyslexia, Wilfred left school without any qualifications. For a number of years he worked as a chef before pursuing a career in television. Unqualified but ambitious and persistent, he talked his way into a job at the BBC, rising to become a producer/director. He is credited with bringing many of the top UK celebrity chefs to the small screen, including Gordon Ramsay, Antony Worrall-Thompson, Brian Turner and James Martin.

In 1994 he founded a food and drink marketing agency in London which went on to run successful marketing campaigns for Loyd Grossman sauces, Kettle Chips, Plymouth Gin, Cobra Beer and other challenger brands.

Wilfred subsequently fulfilled a lifelong ambition and bought a small farm in Devon in 2000. This inspired him to develop and launch The Black Farmer, his hugely successful food brand that includes gluten-free sausages, bacon, chicken, burgers, meatballs, cheese and eggs. The range is sold online and in high-street supermarkets and his signature pork sausages remain one of the country's leading brands of super premium sausages. He has also written *The Black Farmer Cookbook*, which was published by Simon & Schuster.

Flavours Without Frontiers, the promise offered by his products, also goes some way to sum up Wilfred's personality. He will not be confined by race, convention or tradition. Wilfred's strong opinions on issues such as rural affairs, justice for small producers and giving young people more opportunity have driven much media attention. In 2005 he launched a rural scholarship scheme through which young people from inner city communities were given the opportunity to experience what it is like to live and work in the rural community. A Channel 4 documentary filming the progress of the youngsters, *Young Black Farmers*, has been widely aired to much acclaim.

Wilfred is a classic entrepreneur and brings his 'anything is possible' attitude to everything he approaches. He is a business mentor and regularly gives motivational talks to young entrepreneurs. He was awarded an Honorary Doctorate of Marketing by Plymouth University in 2012.

JEOPARDY

WILFRED EMMANUEL-JONES

piatkus

PIATKUS

First published in Great Britain in 2018 by Piatkus

1 3 5 7 9 10 8 6 4 2

A CIP catalogue record for this book
is available from the British Library.

ISBN 978-0-349-41926-8

Typeset in Stone Serif by M Rules
Printed and bound in Great Britain by
Clays Ltd, Elcograf S.p.A

Papers used by Piatkus are from well-managed forests
and other responsible sources.

Piatkus
An imprint of
Little, Brown Book Group
Carmelite House
50 Victoria Embankment
London EC4Y 0DZ

An Hachette UK Company
www.hachette.co.uk

www.improvementzone.co.uk

CONTENTS

Introduction

I had been gone for thirty years, but it was still there: a battered, forlorn structure, with only a smattering of the original blue paint remaining. The door had come off its hinges and was lying on the ground; the roof's tar-black asphalt had been overtaken by mossy green. It looked like the worst-kept garden shed in the world. Still, to me it represented everything.

I am back in the Yardley Wood allotments in Small Heath, Birmingham, where I grew up; a place of poverty and misery that scarred and inspired me in equal measure. It has been decades since I left, vowing never to return. Then, I was a poor, dyslexic, black youngster in a Britain where racism and intolerance were still the norm. Now, returning with a television crew in tow, I am an entrepreneur and a land owner – and someone wants to turn my story into a documentary.

The filmmakers persuaded me to return and, despite my reluctance, I am glad to be back, because this was where it all began – the one place of hope among all the dirt and deprivation of my upbringing. As soon as I enter the allotment I am navigating by memory, ten years old again and back with my father, building the shed that was his pride and joy, and my one place of refuge. This was where I spent countless afternoons in the closest thing to a green space that inner-city Birmingham could offer, learning about crops and simply enjoying the space to move and breathe. As one of nine siblings in a two-up two-down terraced house, space was one of my great luxuries.

It was on that allotment that I made promises to myself that would guide the course of the rest of my life. It was there that I decided I had to get out of the place where I had grown up and escape the life that seemed predetermined for me. And it was there that the dream to own a farm – a real one, not this poky excuse for a paradise – first entered my head. As I will explain in this book, that dream was the driving force that made everything else possible. It was the starting point for a life that has led me from a deprived part of 1960s Birmingham to a beautiful corner of the Devon countryside; which saw me leave school without qualifications at sixteen, but go on to work for the BBC, travel the world making food documentaries and establish two successful companies, including The Black Farmer, a fresh produce business with annual sales in the millions.

Back on the allotment all those years ago, as I helped my dad to paint that shed, I could never have known I would achieve all of this. But I knew I wanted something else, something bigger, something entirely outside the miserable life I knew. Four decades later, my return confirmed that this was the place where the seeds were planted.

How did I achieve these dreams? Indeed, how does anyone transcend their circumstances to change their life for the better? This book is devoted to answering those questions. In all our lives, there are so many different things that contribute to success. No single ingredient can magically erase your troubles and turn your dreams into reality. This book does not claim to provide a silver bullet to success. Instead it offers a key that unlocks the potential to succeed in all of us, regardless of age, background or experience. That key is a mindset we all need if we want to chase our dreams and live the life we always wanted: it is to have the courage to embrace jeopardy.

Jeopardy is the single greatest catalyst for making things happen in life. Where there is jeopardy, there is change, opportunity and possibility. It is the difference between muddling through life and being truly alive; where the world around you is not the drab, repetitive place that it can be, but full of new and exciting things.

Most people associate jeopardy with perilous situations and they are right to do so. What I am advocating here is taking a riskier approach to life than many people would naturally choose to. This is difficult but necessary, because our instinct to be cautious is one of the great barriers to making progress in life. It means we focus on protecting what we already have, rather than expanding our horizons and extending our reach. We might see opportunities and possibilities, but we convince ourselves that the risk of pursuing them is too great. We live life in defensive mode, looking inwards rather than outwards, remaining closed to the world. We think we are safeguarding ourselves, but in reality we are holding ourselves back, stifling our potential.

Conversely, if you accept and seek out jeopardy, you

open the door to opportunity. This means being less comfortable or less secure in order to go further. It means trying things that you are not confident will work. And it means putting yourself in unfamiliar situations that force you to grow and get better in order to succeed.

Jeopardy is not about an easier life, but a better and more fulfilling one – the kind you have always wanted to live. I wish I could say that it's possible to realise your dreams without getting off the sofa, but that isn't the case. However easy some people may make it look, no one really succeeds without serious commitment and a healthy appetite for risk.

To move forward in life, regardless of your goal, you need to embrace jeopardy. Rather than shying away from risk and uncertainty you must acknowledge that they are fundamental components of life and essential ingredients for success. You cannot reap the benefits without first undertaking the challenge. You will never achieve what you really want until you are prepared to tangle with jeopardy.

Improving your odds in the game of life

This message is particularly relevant today because our unprecedented access to information has resulted in the widespread misconception that we can predict the future with certainty; that data will unlock all of the world's mysteries and that we simply have to crunch the numbers and push the buttons to succeed. It is a seductive but ultimately false promise. As much as we may be able to predict, we can never truly know what is going to happen next. If we spend our time worrying about the future and fixating on things we cannot control, then we are simply wasting time and energy. Instead, you should focus your energy on the one thing you *do* have power over: yourself and your attitude to life. Things are going to happen that you can never foresee or expect; the world is going to change around you. But in the midst of this maelstrom, one thing that cannot be taken away from you is your own resilience and self-confidence.

The dictionary says that the word jeopardy derives from the French phrase *jeu parti*, a divided game in which there is an even chance of success or failure. That is the real message of this book. In the game of life, it so often feels like the odds are stacked against you, but they're not. You are just as likely to win as you are to lose, as long as you put yourself in a position to succeed by embracing jeopardy, seeking out new opportunities and equipping yourself with the necessary skills to exploit them. Think of yourself as an athlete in training for the Olympics: only those with ruthless focus and boundless commitment ultimately stand on the podium. Success does not happen by accident: you have to plan for it, work for it and, often, go through hell to make it happen.

We do not live in a world of shortcuts and easy answers. There is only one foolproof route to success that I know: cultivate risk, embrace adversity and uncertainty, and give full expression to your dreams and passions, regardless of how untenable they may seem. Maintain faith and a positive attitude and you will give yourself the best possible chance of succeeding in the end.

A life of jeopardy can be terrifying, but it is always exhilarating. It is uncertain, but full of intent. And it is risky, but not nearly as dangerous as playing it safe. If you want to realise your dreams then jeopardy must be the starting point. If that thought sends a shiver down your spine and makes you feel a little afraid, then get used to it. Embrace it. For without any fear in your life, you have become complacent, comfortable and unchanging. With it, you've got a chance of doing something.

With those butterflies fluttering in your stomach, let us begin.

CHAPTER 1

Embrace jeopardy

In 1910, a baby born in the UK had a life expectancy of between fifty-one and fifty-five years. That same baby, born in 2037, is expected to live on average to the age of ninety-four. And that is just the average. We are getting to the stage where living to a hundred and beyond will no longer be something warranting a telegram from the monarch, but an entirely commonplace event.

Even within the lifetimes of people reading this book – and not just older readers – there have been so many advances in technology, medical science and human knowledge that our wellbeing is now protected in ways that would have been unthinkable for our parents and grandparents. Of course, new technology and longer lives bring their own problems with them. But, fundamentally, there has never been a safer or more prosperous time to be alive. Global levels of extreme poverty and deadly disease have never been lower. Murder rates have plummeted.

Only a committed luddite could ever pretend these developments were anything except wonderful examples of progress and human ingenuity. But such progress does not necessarily come without a price. Because we are not just empirically safer and more prosperous, we are also better protected from the realities of life and death.

I remember as a child accompanying my mother to the Caribbean food markets outside the Bull Ring shopping centre in Birmingham, where the produce was inspected with forensic care and the negotiations were ritually fierce. In those days you could still buy a whole chicken with its feathers on and guts intact. Today, most of us would buy the same animal wrapped up, washed and gutted, and often already jointed for us. We're told that this is safer and healthier, though you only need to look at recent scandals around battery farming and chicken manufacturing to know that it is probably not the case. This may be a small example, but it is perhaps telling of the growing distance between many people and life's harsh truths. This is not only about an appreciation of where our food comes from. You could say the same about how our over-reliance on technology and smartphones is driving people to live more fully in virtual worlds than they do in the real one. We risk not only encasing our relationship with food in plastic, but our entire approach to life. Our self-preservation instincts, designed for a world more immediately dangerous than the one we live in today, can hold us back from taking the risks we need to in order to move forward.

In countless small ways, society is enabling and encouraging us to strip out jeopardy and cocoon ourselves in the comfortable, safe and on-demand world that we have created. There is nothing wrong with all that convenience and efficiency, but it becomes a problem if we are then reluctant to step beyond it. We need to think about whether our safer, more regulated society is stopping us from doing the things we need to make progress in life. This matters, because without some element of danger, and often plenty of it, there cannot be real success. Businesses and careers do not grow without the people behind them pushing beyond what they think is reasonable or possible. There is simply no avoiding risk if you want to achieve big dreams in life. In fact, it is the other way around. It is only by taking risks, by embracing jeopardy and letting it into your life, that you can achieve the things you truly want.

The entire argument of this book is that jeopardy cannot be a foreign country to which you never travel. And it must not be something that you look upon with trepidation. If you spend your life afraid of jeopardy and trying to keep it at bay, it becomes your enemy – the force preventing you from doing the things that can help you make progress. If you embrace jeopardy, however, it can be your friend, propelling you on and helping you overcome the obstacles in your path.

Jeopardy is not something we should look on as a bitter medicine that needs to be swallowed. Rather, it is a wonderful elixir that contains everything you need to succeed. Living with risk sharpens the mind, making you open to opportunities that you might not otherwise have noticed. And if it introduces you to difficult situations you might once have avoided, it also equips you better to overcome these and all the other challenges you will inevitably face.

The greatest myth of all is that jeopardy is something we can avoid, if only we are careful enough in how we go about our daily lives. That is not the choice that you have. We will *all* face danger, fear and loss. The question is not *whether* you will encounter these things. It is how will you respond. The real choice is between being someone who embraces jeopardy, who uses it as the powerful tool it is to unlock personal and life potential, or being the person who shrinks away from it. The latter often think they are in control, whereas in reality they are the ones being controlled. It is the people who accept jeopardy, venturing out into the unknown and exploring the uncertain, who really have the closest thing there is to control over their future. You can never hope to achieve success unless you are first prepared to risk failure. We can never control everything, but each one of us can govern what our attitude to life will be, and how we will approach the challenges and opportunities that we are dealt.

Making things happen

The way many of us live in advanced economies today, the only real experience of jeopardy we have is through a television or computer screen. As science and technology have stripped out much of the risk intrinsic to human life, they have also pushed it into the realm of entertainment. In a country like the UK, most of us experience the worst things in life as performance art, something we can switch off at the touch of a button.

If you are happy with the life you have, entirely fulfilled

in your job and career, succeeding in every ambition you ever had, then that may be fine. Not everyone needs to make a change. But for those who still want to move forward with their lives, to get a better job or make something of the idea that has been in their head for years, some of that jeopardy needs to be reclaimed from the land of entertainment. We need to make it real, to live with it and learn from it.

It starts with this question: are you living the life you really want, or the one that others want for you? That is one of the hardest and most fundamental issues we all face. What do we want to do and who do we want to become? Some people spend their whole lives trying to answer that question, while for others it has been clear for as long as they can remember. In either case, jeopardy is needed: either to discover the life you really want to live, or to fulfil the dream you have always held onto.

Let us be honest: great things in life are not accomplished by sitting in your office, having the same supermarket lunch as you do every day, and hoping that some act of God will rescue you from this tedium. I did not get out of the kitchens I worked in as a young man by hoping I was going to be magically rescued. I worked for it, set myself a daunting goal to enter the entirely unknown world of television and put myself in many uncomfortable positions to achieve that ambition. By doing so, I laid the foundations to eventually achieve my ultimate dream of becoming a farmer and business owner.

The unfortunate truth is that few of the things we want most in life are easily accomplished. Whether it is raising children, building a business or having a virtuoso career, the important things require buckets of stamina and resolve. There will be many times when you think that you are failing and feel ready to give up. Sometimes it is only by carrying on against the odds that you can reach a successful conclusion.

Jeopardy is essential to all enterprises, whether personal or professional. There is as much risk in starting a new relationship as there is in launching a start-up. Taking a chance on someone might be the most wonderful, brilliant thing you have ever done – or it could all end in tears and recrimination. But you won't know until you've tried it. You'll never find out how good something might be until you've exposed yourself to the pain and suffering that all these things risk.

The truth is that life can be extraordinarily exciting and it can also be crushingly dull. Most of us go through periods of experiencing both. I have done jobs that made my mind numb with boredom, as I am sure have many of you reading this. The important thing is that I never saw those things as a resting place. They were always the means to an end. I never stopped holding onto the idea that things could be better and that I had the power to make them so. It is not enough to simply wish change upon yourself. To move from one of these states to the other, to get past things that bore you and reach the ones that you find interesting, you need to go through jeopardy. The exciting jobs and the big opportunities don't fall to people who aren't prepared to risk something to get there. You have to put yourself out there and risk making a bit of an idiot of yourself before anyone is going to notice you or take you seriously. You have to take risks before you can expect to reap rewards. Everyone has to pitch their first product, staff their first professional kitchen service, fly their first plane or write their first article – in whatever field you choose, there is going to be a milestone that feels full of jeopardy as you approach it. There is no escaping it, so it's far better to embrace it, to grab hold of the opportunity and see how far it can take you.

Choosing your own destiny

There is an old debate in the business world about whether entrepreneurs are 'born or made'. Are their talents innate, or developed through experience and persistence? Is it nature or nurture? I have always found the argument somewhat meaningless. No one was calling me an entrepreneur when I was being a pain in the arse at school in Birmingham, or knocking round kitchens as just another commis chef. And I didn't own a business of my own until my late thirties; if it really had been destiny from birth, it took me a bloody long time to get round to it.

No, the idea that we are born to do something, or born unable to do something, is ridiculous. Instead, we are shaped by our circumstances and how we respond to them. Though I didn't think about it at the time, I probably did start to become entrepreneurial at quite a young age, because I looked around me and decided I wasn't going to settle for this life, just following in the footsteps of my parents. I knew I could do better. I had that desire to escape, to make change happen in my life, and that, more than anything, has driven me ever since.

I was only able to achieve that escape because I chased jeopardy. I put myself into situations for which I had no proper training or preparation; I went up against people who were far more qualified than me; and I kept on throwing myself into unknown circumstances to achieve the things I wanted – from the worlds of television to business ownership, farming and, briefly, even politics. My life is one that began with the jeopardy of poverty, a trap I was only able to elude by continuing to pursue risk in everything I have done.

My story could all too easily have been written another way. People where I came from were destined to end up in dead-end jobs at best, prison if they were unlucky or the morgue at worst. But a poor start in life is not a life sentence; it is something that can be overcome, difficult as that may be.

The real trap in my life was not poverty, but victimhood. What decided my fate was not the place or circumstances I was born into, but my response to those things. If I had decided that the world was fated to be against me because I was poor, black, dyslexic and written off, then that is exactly how it would have turned out. But I didn't feel sorry for myself. I got angry instead. And I became determined to show that all the people who had told me that I was thick and a waste of space were wrong. With that sort of motivation, and with a childhood of experiencing jeopardy behind me, chasing uncertainty was never going to feel that daunting. No job interview, sales meeting or investment pitch can ever really seem that terrifying when you know it is helping to prevent you from returning to the bottom of the pile.

We tend to place a lot of importance on people's backgrounds, focusing on whether they were born privileged or not. It's true that the statistics will show that race and poverty have a significant impact on whether you will be well educated, get a good job, enjoy good physical and mental health and stay out of the criminal justice system. There are damaging and disturbing racial disparities in the UK, which require urgent attention. I do not diminish that for a second, and, indeed, I have worked hard to try and open doors for young people of colour in the sectors I operate in: agriculture and retail.

Yet none of that can ever take away the ability of the individual to transcend their circumstances, or to turn an adverse situation to their advantage. If you wanted to argue whether someone born affluent is better placed to become a successful entrepreneur than someone who is born poor, I could make the case either way. If you are from a wealthy family, then you are likely to have some in-built advantages in your favour, whether that is a network of contacts, friends-and-family finance, or the confidence and polish that comes with an expensive education. It's all in your favour, or at least that's how it might seem.

If you were born poor, you probably won't have any of those things. On the surface, it will seem as if you are completely disadvantaged and ill-equipped to succeed. But you will have one thing that more privileged people do not, and that is the desperate desire to succeed, the imperative to do well that comes from knowing what it is like to have no money and not enough food on the table. This is the real hunger possessed only by those who have known what life's dustbin heap looks like. Because you already know what it means to live with jeopardy, you are better placed to seek it out and thrive in your professional life.

So, which is better? The truth is, it doesn't matter if you don't let it. You are the one who decides what sort of life you are going to live. A leg-up early in life can make a big difference, but it isn't necessary. If it were, there wouldn't be so many stories of successful people who came from nothing. We all need help along the way – of course we do – and I have benefited as much as anyone from mentors and guardian angels who helped to pave the way for me. But I would never have found those people had I not gone looking for them, showing my willingness to overcome the circumstances of my birth. You cannot expect anyone to help you unless you are first willing to help yourself.

There is still a lot to be said for the power of the individual. In fact, there is everything to be said for it. And that is true whatever your circumstances or stage in life. My message is, don't buy into the myth of god-given talents and glass ceilings. Don't think of successful people as members of some special breed that you will never be able to equal. Don't fall for the act that some people put on of gliding through life, when the truth is that we all find it hard. Don't get put off pursuing the things you want because others tell you it can't be done. It's natural to feel intimidated by people who look more comfortable, and seem to find everything in life that bit easier, than the rest of us.

But that can only ever be wasted energy. You must focus instead on the things that you have the power to decide – and the most important of these is your willingness to let in jeopardy: to take risks others recoil from, and to embrace a life filled with uncertainty.

People who are willing to take chances can overcome any number of perceived disadvantages, because they place themselves outside the system; they do not depend upon it and its whims. You cannot become the victim of the system if you choose to live outside of it, setting your own rules and following a path of your own creation. So many people live their lives forever focusing on the external: what is going on around them, what other people are doing and what things might happen to them. That really is nothing more than a distraction technique, because the greatest insights come when we look inwards, scrutinising our own capabilities and ambitions, and taking personal responsibility for making them happen. That is one of the hardest but most important things you can do.

Life is not about destiny, but choice. The power to control the future is there for those who choose to take it. There is no guarantee that your journey will be easy, that you will succeed or get what you want. I'm not going to sell you some mumbo jumbo about the doors of opportunity flying open if only you wish it so – guardian angels may exist, but only fairy tales guarantee a happy ending every time. Instead, I am going to share with you the story of my life – from being a poor boy in Birmingham to a landowner and entrepreneur in Devon – and the lessons I have learned along the way. And I am going to explore the two very simple beliefs that have made that journey possible. The first is that every person has the power to set the course of their future life; whatever your circumstances, no one can take that essential ability to self-determine away from you and do not let anyone ever tell you otherwise. The second is that you give yourself the best chance of success if you embrace jeopardy, turning risk and uncertainty from things that you fear into forces through which you can thrive. This book tells you how to do that, explains the advantages this approach offers, and describes the tools it will equip you with to overcome obstacles and succeed.

There's no avoiding it

Jeopardy is all around us. It is inescapable across everything we do, whether at work or at home. We can never be sure when something is about to change unexpectedly, or to go wrong in a way that seriously affects us. We are all going to experience risk, whether we like it or not, and however much we prepare to avoid it. Mistakes will be made, people will get ill, and we will experience painful bereavement and loss. Whatever your attitude towards it, and whether you recognise it or not, jeopardy is a fundamental part of the human existence. Because we cannot avoid it, we must learn to make the best of it.

Even in today's world, safer by so many measures than in previous generations, there is no avoiding the fundamental jeopardy of things that can hurt or harm us. The idea that jeopardy can be bypassed is not simply wrong but actively harmful to our prospects, because it chips away at the mindset vital to achieving the things you want. When you try to close down risks, you are also closing off opportunities. If you are afraid you might not be up to a new job offer that also holds great interest for you, then you are likely to turn it down rather than risk it going wrong. If you worry more about why your business idea might fail than you consider how it might succeed, you are never going to cross the bridge from thinking about it to actually doing it. And if you are paralysed by the fear of rejection, then it is unlikely that you will pluck up the courage to ask someone you like out on a date.

Seeking to avoid risk is both a delusion – because it cannot be averted forever – and an attitude that will inhibit your ability to achieve the things you want most. All of the things we value most in life – falling in love, succeeding in our work, achieving our dreams – rely on an essential dose of courage. None of them can be achieved without trying things that might fail and stepping onto ground that might give way beneath your feet. That is the joy and the agony of being human. The things we most want are always a little out of reach, and sometimes way beyond our grasp. We have to move towards them, and away from the place of certainty that we crave, to reach them.

You can stay in that place of safety. You can minimise the risks you take, and your exposure to being wrong and experiencing failure. But the more you do that, the more you cling to the familiar and push away the uncertain, the smaller your world becomes. Opportunities will pass you by: to seek promotion, change career, start relationships or pursue personal ambitions. Through attempting to avoid risks, you actually create another: the risk that life ends up becoming a series of could-haves, would-haves and should-haves. The danger of holding back is that you are left empty-handed and unfulfilled. And, of course, whatever you do, you cannot escape the jeopardy that affects every life. There is no getting away from jeopardy in our lives, but you can certainly head down a road that ensures you fail to take advantage of the great opportunities life holds.

The opposite mentality is to embrace risk, to live and breathe it in every aspect of your life, from the personal to the professional. A life lived with jeopardy does not have to be about jumping out of planes, scaling tall buildings or crossing high wires. It can be about very normal, everyday things. It is not so much the 'what' that matters, as the 'how': how you choose to approach your everyday life, how you think about the future, how you go about seeking to achieve your dreams.

A person who lives with jeopardy is someone who fundamentally accepts that good things can only be achieved through risk and uncertainty. They are not afraid to try things that they do not know about, or may not be able to do. They do not worry about looking foolish in front of their peers. They are happy to be proved wrong, if that ultimately helps them to learn something and get it right next time. Their focus is not on the nonsense and politics of how things look, but on what works and what helps them to achieve the things they want. What they do fear is having a life that fails to live up to its potential, of passing up on opportunities to do big and exciting things, and of finally retreating to their pipe and slippers feeling unfulfilled. For these people, the real danger in life comes not in action but inaction. The real fear is of not achieving what you wanted from life. The real failure is in not trying at all.

Perhaps the best way to begin understanding jeopardy is to think about when you fell in love for the first time. How you felt your heart beat and the blood pump. The anticipation and the excitement. The fear and the joy all mixed together. That sick feeling in the pit of your stomach. That is jeopardy, a step into the unknown, one that could trip you up, but something that could also change your life.

Now think about your everyday life and work. Does it make your heart beat faster and leave you with that tingling sensation? For many people, the answer will be no. You do the things that are familiar, in a way that you know will work. You avoid things that could lead to mistakes and seek consensus rather than pursuing an idea that others have discounted. It is about the comfort of the familiar and the safety of the pack; it is about keeping danger at bay, locked away in its box.

There is another way, and that is the way of jeopardy. Trying things that might, and often will, fail. Going ahead, even when all the people you trust are telling you not to. Having a go, even when the odds against you seem daunting. And keeping going, even when you can't immediately see a way to succeed. If you want to build a successful business or career, whatever your field, you will need to do all those things. You will have that sick feeling in your stomach often. You won't always succeed and sometimes you will fail decisively. But you will give yourself the chance of success, and that is really all we can ever do. You can't control what other people are going to say, think or do. Your idea might not work, your request might not be granted, or the timing may not be right for your particular venture. You can guarantee and predict none of these things. But you can control your attitude, your actions and your intent. And you can choose to put yourself in the game, whatever that may be, by embracing uncertainty. The other choice is to remain stuck on the sidelines, looking on but unable to participate. Only by accepting jeopardy do you ever get onto the field in the first place.

Exiting the comfort zone

I can understand that some of you reading this may accept the idea of jeopardy, but not feel that you are the kind of person who can readily embrace it. I believe this is another common misconception. In the same way that we regard successful people as somehow apart, we often fall into the trap of thinking that risk-takers are a select group, one completely different from the rest of us. We consider risk to be the domain of others, a place only for daredevils or those who have nothing to lose. Much easier to stay in our corner, where we are protected from failure and harm.

That is wrong, wrong, wrong. Risk is necessary for everyone, whether you imbibe it in small or large doses. It could be quitting your job to pursue the business or life dream you have always nurtured. Or it could be as simple as going to your boss and asking for the promotion or pay rise that is long overdue and that you know you deserve. Both take some guts and resolve to do. Both require risking something, whether that is your livelihood or just a relationship with an individual colleague or manager. But unless we take those risks, we are forever going to be sitting about wondering what would have happened if we had been a little bit braver. Jeopardy doesn't have to be about taking giant leaps the whole time and it doesn't have to mean betting the house or becoming a daredevil. It can be something you start to embrace in all sorts of small ways that will help you to move forward in your career and in life.

Those first steps are the hardest, but once you have taken them, I can almost guarantee that you will start to feel a difference. Jeopardy does not stop after the first taste of uncertainty. Once you've tried a little, you won't want to stop. Once the first risk has paid off, why not try another one? And once the first big failure has been experienced, the prospect of getting it wrong again doesn't seem so bad. By experiencing jeopardy you are proving to yourself that you can succeed or fail, and still live to tell the tale. You see that the risks aren't as big as you perhaps thought, and that the reality of being wrong isn't so bad after all. When you've got used to people saying no to your ideas, had the edges knocked off you and started to experience the ups and downs of a life that is lived with uncertainty, you become battle hardened. You're prepared for what life has to throw at you and the many challenges that will come your way when pursuing big ambitions.

The moment you force yourself out of your comfort zone and realise how much is out there, you won't want to go back into your cocoon. Why limit your world, when there is so much out there to discover and experience? Isn't narrowing your sights the greater risk than broadening them?

Jeopardy, then, is necessary to start pursuing new opportunities in your life and career. But it is more than just that. It is also the way we learn – about ourselves and other people, about what we are really capable of and how to get the things we want. Only when we live on the edge of what we think possible do we truly discover the extent of our potential.

Of course, the opposite to living on the edge – in business, as in life – is being stuck in the comfort zone. This may seem like a place of security, but it is also one of stasis, where things are defined by their ability to stay the same. This appearance of safety can be a deceptive one. For what feels secure today can easily become outdated and unsustainable tomorrow. Nothing should ever be taken for granted or assumed to be unchangeable, yet people who live and work in the comfort zone are never ready for that change because they are depending upon it never happening. That is the risk of trying to create certainty in a fundamentally uncertain world. Living with jeopardy is not just about embracing the need for change; it is about enhancing your own ability to thrive in times of change.

We can only succeed in life when we grow as people, and that only happens through encountering new challenges, new circumstances and new experiences. In other words, by taking chances. If the last time you felt really nervous at work was on your first day, then I will venture that you are probably not pushing yourself hard enough. Jeopardy is not just something you need to embrace, it is also your personal pressure gauge: if you're feeling it, then that's good and you are doing something right, even if you're not quite sure what comes next. If you're not feeling it, then you really need to ask yourself why not.

It comes back to the question of whether you want your life to be exciting or not. Jeopardy is what achieves that. The reason we love stories is because of the element of risk they explore: turning the pages to find out what happens next, whether the characters we have invested in will make the right decisions and get the things they seek. We continue to read books and go to the cinema because the best authors and filmmakers create doubt. They make their stories about flawed personalities and difficult decisions; and we hang on every word to see how it is going to conclude. That is jeopardy, and we need the same thing in our own lives too: a life lived with jeopardy is more exciting, more rewarding and filled with more opportunity. This is something within the grasp of everyone, however you might initially feel. Society may be stripping out natural risk, but that does not mean you have to follow suit. You can let jeopardy into your life and make a conscious decision to pursue the full limits of what you are capable of achieving. I don't pretend that this will be easy, but what it will do is mean a life and career in which you will have no regrets about the things you didn't do, the opportunities that you weren't bold enough to pursue.

Throughout this book, I alternate chapters that look at the challenges that jeopardy throws up (such as fear, risk, uncertainty and adversity) with the advantages of jeopardy – from dreams to passion, faith and hope. It is my hope that these examples will help more people to see what there is to gain from embracing risk in their lives.

Every packet of Black Farmer sausages ever produced has carried the same promise printed on it: 'Flavours without Frontiers'. That means that we deliver what we think are the best sausages in the world and we let nothing dilute that vision. We don't economise on time or ingredients. We do everything in service of the best flavour: no cost-cutting or compromises that would undermine the belief in best. In the same way, I believe that we all have the chance to live a life without frontiers. We can free ourselves from the shackles that inhibit the way we think and make decisions. We can do more than we initially think ourselves capable of. And we can take on the people and competitors who try to stand in our way. We can do all this. Nobody is stopping us except ourselves. And if you're asking whether you can do it, then I'd ask you to consider this: you have actually been living with jeopardy since the very moment you arrived in this world. Being born is a dangerous enough thing in itself. Staying alive and keeping your head above water is bloody hard too, and you've made it this far. Why not try and go a little further?

CHAPTER 2

Stop surviving

Jeopardy matters. You are with me so far, and there's a lot further still to go. Throughout this book I explore the many ways in which we can embrace jeopardy in our lives, the decisions we will have to make, the circumstances that this approach will introduce us to and the techniques for dealing with the challenges that a life full of uncertainty brings. I want to demonstrate how the power of jeopardy can be harnessed to pursue life dreams and unlock personal potential. But before we can start to do that, there is something else to discuss, something that is really essential if any of the rest of my advice is going to matter: recognising the kind of person you really are.

This isn't about what you do for a living or where you've come from in life. Everything in this book can apply to pretty much everyone, regardless of their wealth, background, race, age or experience. My point is about something more fundamental: your underlying personality, your instincts and the way you consciously and unconsciously approach every decision in life. Now there are all sorts of clever psychological metrics that can tell you whether you're an extrovert or an introvert, commanding or consensus-driven, and so on. But I am no scientist and I am going to try and simplify it. Based on my experience, there are basically two kinds of people in this world. Survivors and outsiders.

Survivors are people whose primary instinct, always, is to repel any threat of danger or harm. They weigh everything by its potential to go wrong, and they see risks as something to be avoided rather than seized upon. Survivors want to maintain the life they have created for themselves, to cling to their comfort zone and ideally never venture beyond it. For them, jeopardy is something to be feared and not loved.

Outsiders are the opposite. They are the people who have welcomed jeopardy into their lives. They do not allow themselves to be defined by the constraints of any company or even society as a whole. Outsiders know that progress only happens when you break from tradition and the status quo. They realise that change is one of the essential components of life, and they embrace that both for themselves and the organisations they are involved in.

As in all these things, there is a sliding scale between the two. You may not be a pure outsider or a complete survivor. Many of us will be a mixture of the two, with some instincts to be bold and others that urge caution. Often the two impulses will be at war with each other as we work through the difficult decisions in our lives and careers, but there can be no doubt that, to fully embrace jeopardy in your life, you need to become more of an outsider and less of a survivor. You need to relinquish some of the instincts that hold you back from being bold, and to acquire the outsider's appetite for subverting the consensus view. There is no absolute transformation from one to the other, but if there is a scale, then you need to tip the balance in favour of your inner outsider. For everyone this will be different, and we are all starting from different places. As they say, however, the first step to solving a problem is to admit you have one – and you are going to struggle to fully embrace jeopardy if your survival instincts remain dominant.

The survivor's mentality

Before those instincts can be addressed, we need to understand where they come from: survival is not a simple psychology, but one of our most essential and basic human instincts. It is the desire to belong, to be part of something, to have others by our side. From the moment we are born, screaming for our mothers, we are instinctively looking to return to a place of comfort and safety, a place where we feel protected from harm. Our need to belong reflects in the friendships that we form at school, the tribes we join around sport, music or fashion, and in our desire to find a companion to share our lives with. It shows up in our fear of being left out or left behind, of being expelled from the club because we fail to keep pace. As children it was about having the right shoes and supporting the same team; as adults it's about tracking our career and life success against friends and peers. Often this is presented as competitiveness, but, fundamentally, it is much more about the desire to blend in than to stand out. We match ourselves against others because status matters, and we all want to know our place in the pecking order, real or imagined.

But what if that instinct is wrong? What if the very thing driving some of our most basic emotions was also the force that is holding us back from the things we most want to achieve? What if our desire to be part of a herd is limiting our potential as individuals? Our survival instincts are deeply ingrained for good reason, but in a world where we are better protected from the realities of life and death than ever before, they can also be counterproductive.

By survivor, I do not mean someone who has necessarily been through some great tragedy, but rather a person whose default state in life is to try and stand still, to preserve what they have and risk nothing. The survivor's mentality is one that is completely at odds with everything I discuss in this book. It is about rejecting jeopardy, running from risk and putting all energies into maintaining the status quo. The survivor builds walls around the life they already have, rather than seeking to break new ground.

For survivors, the future is something to be feared rather than anticipated. They worry about what is going to happen and what they stand to lose. The fear of making mistakes, the desire to mitigate risk and an aversion to taking responsibility are their key traits. As individuals, the survival mentality reveals itself when we say no to something because we fear we might not be good enough to succeed. Our fear of failure, aversion to being embarrassed and having our flaws revealed means that we sometimes choose to survive in our comfort zone rather than venture out into less certain territory where our credibility, financial security and sense of self are at risk.

An obvious home for the survival mentality is government. Step inside one of the departments that is running our country and you will see what it really means to fear the future. These are places where, however many brilliant people you put in (and there are lots of good ones), the overall culture is entirely based on avoidance of mistakes or of accountability for outcomes. They plan for things to go wrong before they even start to think what success would look like. The bureaucracy that these places thrive on is death to the outsider mentality. It squeezes out jeopardy at every conceivable opportunity, always seeking a safer option, always covering its back against the possibility of failure or criticism. And when you are doing that, you make it very hard to actually do anything of substance.

You see a lot of this same mentality in big business too. Companies that were once outsiders with youth and energy on their side get fat and complacent as they become established. They grow into the incumbents that they had once stood against. All the old dynamism is eroded by that same fear factor, the same instinct to hoard your gains and protect against future losses. When you have a lot to lose, then survival starts to become the name of the game. And it is then that, as an individual or organisation, you need to start worrying. Because the moment you are trying to defend yourself rather than go on the attack is the moment when you lose the precious gift of forward momentum. You have become the Romans with the barbarians at the gate, and we all know how that ended.

There is another trait shared by survival institutions, both political and corporate. They are all run on the essential basis of fear, a mindset that looks not towards what can be gained, but what is about to be lost. That fear begins at the top of an organisation and trickles down to all levels until you have a chain of command along which everyone is afraid of their superior and pushes that fear down the hierarchy onto the next person who reports to them. As I discovered when working with food and drinks companies as a marketer, this means that much of what goes on in business is analysed not on its merits, but through the prism of what someone's boss or their boss's boss will think about it. Better a bad idea that doesn't rock the boat than a good one that might. In fact, probably better to do nothing at all, to just keep things as they are.

This fear of what might happen if something changes dominates organisations of this kind. That is why you will find them stuffed full of processes and other things dreamed up to create an outward impression of order. This is our curiously human way of trying to control what we never can: the world that is always changing around us. We cannot know. We cannot predict the future, so instead we plan, we build systems and we cling to them as to the port in a storm. Survival is not just the broad mentality at the heart of big business and government, to name just two areas; it is an entire thought system with a huge amount of ballast and process behind it. Entire careers are committed not to the pursuit of progress, but to obstructing it. Every good idea is also a threat to an existing process or person, and the tendency to try and crush it will often be stronger than the instinct to nurture it.

If you are someone who has worked within one of these institutions, and that is probably most of us who have had multiple jobs, then you have seen and experienced all this first hand. It may even have rubbed off on you. People become survivors, stuck in their jobs and stale in their careers, when they allow institutional fear – conscious or otherwise – to take over and direct the way they think. It becomes easier not to question things, not to strive for the very best outcome, but simply to fall into line and to do as others do, settling for an easy life rather than pursuing an exciting one.

If you're not sure, then ask yourself this. Are you still thinking about what you want to achieve with your life, about big dreams you want to fulfil? Or are you more focused on getting through to the end of the week until you can crash on the sofa or go to the pub? There is a difference between living and merely existing. Being alive is about more than getting up in the morning; it is about having a purpose to your life that keeps you going and gives you that inner energy and spirit. To merely exist is a fatiguing, unfulfilling experience, where you are happier when the day is over than when it is about to begin. And that is survival mode: doing the minimum, keeping your head down and hoping no one notices.

Survival mode is not usually a choice that people make; it is one of those things that creeps up – as we lose momentum in our careers, as family needs and other demands pile up – and it becomes hard to look beyond next week, let alone to think about what you want to be doing for the next twenty years. It is something that slowly but surely descends as we get comfortable to the point of boredom doing the same old things, no longer having to prove ourselves but just going around the same circuit again. Life is tiring and it gets tempting to settle for what we have, to set down the dreams we may have once held, and to get on with the job of working, parenting and surviving another week.

Some people are happy to do so, and I do not want to criticise that. No one should be maligned for the kind of life they choose to live; this is not about one thing being better or worse than the other but about what you actually want for yourself. And I believe that too many people do not get to live the life they would ideally choose. I have written this book because I think there are many who are not happy and who are looking for a way out of the quicksand they have found themselves in. A lot of people are stuck in jobs they do not find fulfilling anymore, if they ever did. A lot of us have dreams that we still want to achieve, even if we have lost sight of how that might be done. I have had moments in my life when I felt stuck and trapped, but equally others where I have managed to race ahead and move towards the things I wanted most. And I want to show other people how they can think about doing the same.

It is possible because, though you might not have chosen to enter survival mode, you do have a choice about what to do next. There is no rule that says you have to accept being stuck with a job that no longer makes you happy. And there is every opportunity to break out of the routine that you may feel stuck in. People can feel powerless to make changes in their life, but only rarely is that actually the case. More often, they have simply lost the will to try, and the hunger to break free. But the means still exist – are there, ready and waiting, if you can shed the mantle of the survivor and embrace your potential as an outsider.

The outsider's mentality

Being an outsider means that, rather than clinging to the known and the familiar, you actively embrace the unknown and the uncertain. Outsiders step beyond the constraints that survivors impose upon themselves. They free themselves to think and work unconventionally, doing the things that others deem unwise or unlikely.

For me, being an outsider was something that came naturally, because I was never someone who naturally belonged in life. I was a pain in the arse at school and left without any proper qualifications. I got kicked out of the army, which in the 1970s wasn't the best fit for a mouthy black git like me. I got my break with the BBC in the 1980s, when it was an almost entirely Oxbridge enclave, and I had never even seen a university, let alone thought of attending one. And I made my name in an industry where I wasn't just unusual, but unique: the UK's only black farmer.

Having never been a natural member or joiner of things, I have a different perspective. It hasn't been something that has held me back. In fact, I see it as one of my greatest strengths. I have always been an outsider, someone who does not fit the mould and is not going to work particularly hard to change that.

The great benefit of being an outsider is that you do not have to follow the rules. People already look at you as an oddity, so who cares if you have a completely different method or opinion on how something should be done? And it is by breaking the rules that we make progress in life. Every great invention and every successful company has diverted from the norm in some way. People have created products that the experts said there would never be an appetite for, and relaunched others whose markets were considered to be long past. Entrepreneurs have gone up against competitors whose incumbency seemed impregnable, but who proved to be entirely fallible. All these things have happened, time and time again, throughout history. The consensus view is forever being proved wrong in almost every field, but that does little to diminish its power and hold over most people.

It is outsiders who have the freedom and self-belief to break with it and try new things. That is the great strength of not belonging: you don't have obligations to the tribe, you don't have to abide by its rules and you don't have to worry about what its other members think. You can just get on with what you think is the right and best thing to do. Just as a convoy travels at the pace of the slowest boats, groups do not progress at the speed of the best ideas they create. They are inflexible, slow-acting and deeply political. When so many different interests need to be taken into account, you end up with compromises rather than serious resolutions. Just as you cannot take effective decisions by committee, you cannot drive powerful ideas forward when you are constrained by the needs of the collective. A survivor cannot be an innovator.

The groups that I describe are often not formal membership organisations, although they can be. Indeed, many of them are invisible, and people are often a part of them without realising it. What I am talking about applies to any kind of cosy consensus, from the way an individual company is run to the principles that entire industries operate under, and the beliefs that people hold. I have seen this at play in worlds as diverse as television, farming and politics. It never ceases to amaze me how consistently so many people sing the same tune at you, and how often that melody is a negative one, resigned to perpetuating an existing situation that people do not like but feel trapped by nonetheless. In politics, it was about the power of the party whips and the need to fall in line; in farming, it has been about the inevitability of decline as low supermarket prices squeeze the life out of small producers. In both worlds, I was told that this is the way the system works and, whether you liked it or not, you had to go along with it. This practised resignation is the battle cry of the survivor and it is poison to people who want to make progress. It may not be easy, but every system can be hacked and every establishment infiltrated. You can find a way in and a path through, if you really want and need to.

It takes an outsider's mind to step away from the prevailing negativity, escape the constraints of the system as it stands and start seeing new opportunities for how things can be done differently. In business, the outsiders are start-ups – young companies who disrupt the system. Unencumbered by the baggage of the past, they undermine established competitors and create whole new industries.

In politics we have seen an age of outsiders, such as Jeremy Corbyn: people who were written off by their opponents as useless, but who tapped into something latent in the public mind.

I believe we can all do more with our lives by accessing that spirit of the outsider: someone who doesn't accept what everyone else tells them, but has the independence of thought and action to come up with their own conclusions. The outsider looks like a lunatic until they have proven something, at which point they become a pioneer and, in many cases (especially if you think of inventors and innovators), an example to follow. Those who succeed will often find that the very same people who denounced their foolishness will become their biggest fans – once it has become safe to do so.

To be an outsider you have to embrace the jeopardy that comes with it. You have to give up the reassurance of having other people who agree with you all the time, and in career terms you will often have to give up the comfort of a steady job and a regular salary. It is not an easy path, but if you pursue it you give yourself a better chance of achieving the things you truly want. Why? Because with the mindset of the outsider, you have freedom. That could be freedom over how you spend your time, freedom about how you can think, freedom with which to explore, experiment and discover. Only with that freedom do you have the scope to fully pursue your dreams, to stop worrying about what might go wrong, and to try and make great things happen in your life.

So many people live lives constrained by their

circumstances. They never step off the path that has been laid out for them, to discover how much they can actually achieve. For those reading this, I want to suggest something different. Nothing is inevitable in life and the book is not closed on you or your future. It is you yourself who has the power to write it. But the first page you must turn to is the one that allows you to escape the strictures that exist within your life, and to embrace the power and the jeopardy of being an outsider.

Escaping survival mode

How do I make a change? It's the question people ask themselves in those idle moments of clock-watching and daydreaming their way through another week at the office. Because it's almost certainly true that many more people want to transform their lives than actually succeed in doing so. You only have to look at the gap between the number of people who say they want to start a business, and those who actually go on to do it.

The reason is that survival mode is seductive. You may have had to work hard to get there, and you could be losing a lot by stepping outside the comfort zone you have created. Dreams about doing something different are enticing, but we know it will be hard to actually go ahead and do it. We all know what we stand to lose if something goes wrong. It's easier to just to keep things the way they are and let our ambitions remain idle fantasies, a nice diversion but nothing more.

There are any number of forces that will try to stop you

from moving out of survival mode. Some are in your own head: your confidence in yourself and your abilities, your unwillingness to put what you have already gained in life on the line. Some are external: the people and influences that tell us we probably can't do it, that we shouldn't risk it and it's going to be too hard to even try. At every turn, there will be better evidence for not making a big change than for doing so. The balance will always fall in favour of staying put rather than venturing outwards. The logical conclusion will invariably be that you should wait and see, play it safe for now and put off ambition for another time.

There is never going to be a moment in your life when all the factors magically align in your favour. The circumstances will never be quite right, you will never know as much as you ideally want to, and you are always going to be untested in some way. That is the fundamental jeopardy of trying to do anything new or exciting in your life. It's always going to be a bloody great risk, and there is no way of insuring yourself against a bad outcome. You can either let that jeopardy be your constant enemy, let it become the permanent reason for inaction, or you can grasp it as an opportunity. Nothing really good in life has ever come without jeopardy, and to get to the places we want to be in life we must leave the safe harbours that we create for ourselves. We have to make jeopardy a positive reason to act, staring it down and understanding the huge advantages it holds when harnessed as a positive life force.

If you are to do that, then you need to step outside your comfort zone, give up the comfort blanket of survival and hand in your membership card to whatever club you have been a part of until now. That could be the company you work for, the friends you grew up with, or the people who came from the same place as you. For me, it was about leaving behind the only two worlds I knew: the inner city of Birmingham and the kitchens where I had started to make my career after being kicked out of the army. They were never places I wanted to stay, and in fact I had long been desperate to get out. But that still did not make it easy to go from a place where you are fundamentally a member of the tribe to one in which you can only ever be an outsider. In my case, it involved swapping the chopping board for the cutting room to build an entirely different career in television. That was something that eventually led me into the world of food, which in turn paved the way to fulfilling my dream of owning a farm and running my own business.

I am not saying that you should never see your friends again, or that you need to renounce your former life and burn the evidence (though if you are going to start your own business, don't expect to see much of your friends for the first few years!). It is a more subtle change than that, one that is about breaking the mindset of what it means to belong, and embracing the refreshing chill of being the outsider. The harsh truth is that you cannot have it both ways – both the comfort of being embraced by familiar people and experiences, and the rush of voyaging into the unknown to achieve new things and pursue your dreams. If you want to chase that dream then you need to become more of the outsider, and you can never do that while you are clinging to the safety of the pack. Achieving the things you want most in life is never easy, and it will almost certainly mean giving up some other things that you value and think you need. The road to success is often a lonely place and there is no point pretending otherwise. You need to embrace the mentality of the outsider early on if you are going to have a chance of making it all the way.

To be or to belong?

Deciding to take on an outsider's outlook may be harder than it sounds, because it first requires a full and frank acknowledgement of where you have reached in life. Many people that I would categorise as survivors would not consider themselves to be in that bracket. They might even be offended by the notion. Yet you have to be honest with yourself. There is no shame in admitting that you have gone off track if you then resolve to do something about it. It is far better to have that honesty than to be in denial because you would rather hide from the truth.

The question you must ask is a simple one, in two parts. The first: what do I want to achieve in my life? And the second: what am I currently doing to contribute towards that end goal? If the answer to that second question is 'nothing', then can you really say you are doing anything else except surviving?

The other way I like to think about it is the difference between being and belonging. If your focus is on the need to belong, if you are a member of the tribe or part of the group, then it is much harder to actually take the strides you need towards success. When you prioritise belonging, your focus is not on what you need to do to make progress, but on forever looking back over your shoulder, thinking of what other people would be doing in the same circumstances and of what the rest of the group thinks about you. It is hard to pursue your dreams when you have the comfort of belonging, which might also be seen as something of an invisible shackle. There are too many things getting in your way and stopping you from focusing on the one thing you need to be thinking about.

By contrast, someone who is willing to *be* has one of the greatest assets in life, and that is focus. That sounds easy enough, but it is not. We live in a world of distractions, with endless sources of information and entertainment competing for our attention. It is harder than ever to simply focus on the goal you are trying to achieve; the clutter and obligations of being a survivor just add to that burden. When you are focused on being, the things you want to achieve and the person you want to become, that is an amazing liberation. Because, with the ability to focus, you can see things clearly: the things you need to do and the challenges that lie ahead of you. Your mind isn't full up with a thousand useless thoughts and concerns, but has the rare clarity on what you need to achieve – today, tomorrow and in the next year. So many of us spend so much of our time on things that do not really matter, letting the white noise of everyday life drown out things that are actually important. It is hard to find focus, but it is essential, and it is only possible by stepping outside our cosy clubs and comfort zones.

By surrendering belonging and choosing to be, you gain the single-mindedness that has been the hallmark of all great achievers in life, from business to politics, the arts and sport. Do you think that people like Roger Federer or Richard Branson achieved their success simply by putting their heads down, and working hard to fit in with those around them? No, they stood out because they had a relentless focus on the task at hand, as well as a ruthless desire to get on and get better. It's the same story if you pick apart the anatomy of any really successful person, in whatever walk of life. Almost all of them will have a real streak of the outsider in them. They didn't think about or do things in the same way as their peers, and they didn't follow the club rules. And in doing so they assumed the great strength of the outsider – the person who chooses to be true to themselves and forget about fitting in with everyone else. They had the singularity of vision and purpose that marks out the great from the good. And that is something we all need to achieve our dreams, whatever they may be.

If that sounds selfish, it's because it is. It would be nice to say to you all that you can succeed in life while being a completely lovely person who always thinks of others before they think of themselves, who is as much committed to their family and friends as they are to work, and who enjoys a perfect work-life balance. But that is simply not the case, however much we might wish it to be. If you want to build a business or be a virtuoso in your chosen field, it is going to take a level of commitment that borders on obsessiveness. You are going to need to put yourself and your project first, tending to its needs and treating it like the most important thing in the world.

That doesn't mean you have to be a horrible person, ignoring your friends and family and becoming selfishly focused on yourself at all costs. But it will mean making some sacrifices and missing out on things you would otherwise want to do. Not many entrepreneurs get to go on holiday every summer, tuck in their kids every night or go to every party they are invited to; at least not when they are in the hard-grafting early years of getting a venture off the ground. An athlete in training can't just forget about their regime and get drunk in the pub because it's their best friend's birthday. There's simply no pretending that there is an easy route to doing things that are hard. It takes commitment, stamina and an unswerving belief that what you are doing matters, and warrants making these sacrifices. To the outsider such self-possession comes naturally, whereas to the survivor it often seems like too much hard work.

What finally defines outsiders is a hunger: to succeed, to prove themselves, to get better and to get on in life. The people who most readily embrace jeopardy are those who are too impatient to play by the rules of the club. They don't want to be members because they can see that it's slowing them down, and they want to march to the beat of their own drum. That has been the mentality of every true entrepreneur in history: the desire to escape the strictures that others place upon them, and to be the ruler of their own universe. In the end, there is no greater thing in life than being the master of your own time and the controller of your own destiny. Not relying on other people to make things happen for you, but taking responsibility for doing it yourself. But you can only do that by becoming an outsider and that is not something that comes without a fundamental dose of jeopardy.

So, you have to ask yourself: do you have that hunger and what are you hungry for? For me, the great motivator was escaping poverty, but hunger can come from all sorts of places and we all have different drivers. It doesn't matter what fuels you, as long as you have that essential desire to achieve something, and the recognition that you must let jeopardy into your life to do so.

You have to be honest with yourself. What do you really want from life and what will actually make you happy? The important thing is to recognise that there is no having one foot in both camps. There is no chasing big dreams without embracing jeopardy and all that it brings with it. You cannot run with the horses and hunt with the hounds, keeping your club membership and being an outsider at the same time. The two are incompatible and you have to choose. In or out. Survivor or outsider. It's one or the other.

Though there is advice here that could apply to almost anyone's life situation, and I think we can all benefit from embracing risk in our lives, this is a book written mainly with outsiders in mind. It's for the people who want to step outside the mainstream to build new things and pursue a different path. That has been the story of my life, and I am going to share what I have learned along the way. But before you get to that, you need a place to start. And that is at the beginning, with the thing that you most of all want to achieve. Your dream.

CHAPTER 3

Dream a dream

It takes a long time to achieve your dreams in life. For me it took almost thirty years. At the age of eleven, I made a promise to myself that has guided the rest of my life, and it wasn't until past my fortieth birthday that I delivered on it. The promise was this: on my father's allotment in inner-city Birmingham, I vowed that one day I would own a real piece of land, a farm, a piece of Britain to call my own – and somewhere a million miles from the misery and poverty of the place where I grew up.

That idea, that dream, has been my guiding light ever since. It has been the inspiration to keep on going through jobs I hated; the retort to people who told me I would never amount to anything; and the source of the burning passion that we all need to succeed in life. It is all very well talking about determination, faith and passion, but you have to have something to be determined and passionate about; something to really believe in. It's the source of those things that makes them so strong; the vision or cause that you are fighting for. And that is why every success story, in every field of human endeavour, starts with a dream.

Dreams are easy to disdain. Many people think they don't need them, that logic and reason should always come first. In business especially, the very idea of dreaming is dismissed as emotion, the irrational impulse that must be put aside, locked away in its box when decisions are being made. The people who believe this are often those who have given up on their own dreams, who no longer pursue a life of ambition but exist in survival mode, as we have just discussed.

It is fine to live like that. Many people do. But if you are ambitious, if you have things you want to achieve and if you want to go further, then you must be a dreamer. With a dream, you have one of the most important things to succeed in life and that is focus: a central purpose you can keep coming back to for inspiration and motivation. Because, despite what life's survivors may think, there is no way of shielding yourself from harm and loss. We all have to suffer what life throws at us; we will all experience setbacks and difficulties. Your dream is what can keep you focused and on track, whatever gets thrown in your path. It is something that nobody and nothing can take away from you. The things that happen to you in life can eat away at your dreams, but they can't destroy them. Only you can finally give up on them. And only you can achieve them.

Dreams are the great leveller. We all have the power to dream; in that moment it doesn't matter whether you are rich or poor, young or old, accepted or discriminated against. In your own head, you can dream about the better life you want to build for yourself. And by doing so you are taking the first step to living that life.

As a young man, growing up poor and black in one of the most deprived areas of the UK, dreams were my refuge from the grinding realities of everyday life. When you are sharing a bed with two other brothers, and a single chicken has to feed a family of eleven, you need a place to get away. My refuge was the allotment, a green space that seemed huge to me as a child when the rest of my world consisted of overcrowded terraced houses and the concrete jungle. The allotment was where I came to get away and to dream, my oasis from inner-city life. It was where I first started to develop a real love for food – not just on the plate, but from the ground – with my father teaching me how to plant vegetables. And it was where the dream that has defined my life began.

A dream to become a farmer doesn't sound like the most aspirational or exceptional thing. It's not like the dream of the kid who says they want to be an astronaut or a Premier League footballer. But in the circumstances of the time, I may as well have said I wanted to go to the moon as own a farm of my own. This was the 1960s, and the reality of being black in Britain was defined by rampant racism and prejudice. At very best, you were expected to become a bus conductor, a hospital porter or a labourer, and to feel lucky that you had a job at all. My father, a highly educated man, found that none of his qualifications or experience counted for anything. He was a proud man, a pastor, which had made him an important community figure in the Clarendon parish of Jamaica where I was born. But he found himself having to take a job in a factory, one that demeaned him, made no use whatsoever of his talents and left him struggling to put enough food on the table. It meant he had to give up on the dream of a better life that had moved him, and so many others in the Caribbean, to make the journey to Britain in the first place.

In that world, the idea of becoming a farmer, a black boy entering a white man's world, was not just audacious but ridiculous. To give you an idea of quite how outlandish it was, consider that, decades later, being a black man owning a Devon farm was still enough of a novelty that I have been able to build my whole brand around the idea. When I moved south in the late 1990s, some of my neighbours had still never met a black person; a few decades earlier, the pitchforks would probably have been out, and that was the prevailing attitude when I first started to talk about my unlikely dream.

Yet it was the very audacity of the dream that made it so lasting and important to me. That is the first thing to consider. If you want to dream, you need to dream big. That doesn't mean your dream should be impossible, or that there can't be plenty of achievable steps along the way. But the dream itself has to be something bold enough that it scares you. The jeopardy of a dream is that it's something you might well never achieve. Anything worth doing comes with the distinct possibility of failure, and if you're not scared of falling short, then you're not reaching far enough in the first place. Your dream, the founding vision in your life, should be something that is significant enough to be carried with you through different jobs,

different places and different stages in your life. It can't be
something you will tick off in a few weeks, and it might be
the work of many years or take even decades to achieve.
It needs to be audacious enough that you will fear it, and
others will refuse to believe it.

Audacity is something that has been a defining feature
of my life. I remember what must have been one of my first
school swimming lessons: our teacher divided us up into
groups of those who already knew how to swim, and the
beginners. I stuck up my hand as one of the swimmers,
even though I had no idea how to swim. I wasn't going to
let that small reality get in the way of showing I was confident. Of course, I got into trouble very quickly and had to
be rescued, but it makes me smile now to think of it. Even
then, I had the audacity to try and pull off things I had no
right to do. And though it didn't help me as a youngster in
the swimming pool, that attitude most certainly did when
it came to advancing my career as a young man.

Your dream needs to be audacious. It should also be
deeply personal. There's no point in saying that you want
to be a novelist, an artist or a chef unless you want to live
and breathe your craft: to devote your life to mastering
it. This is about dreams rooted in your sense of self, your
passions and your ambitions in life. My dream to own a
farm was born out of my childhood love of open spaces
and the outdoors. Growing up in a house where we lived
three to a bed, I was so used to cramped conditions that
being outdoors, in the land, has always meant a great deal
to me. And if my father's allotment was a small taster of
what that could be like, then I always knew I wanted the

real thing. If the outdoors was my passion, my ambition was even simpler: to get out of the place where I grew up and to never look back.

Having a big dream, from such an early stage in life, helped me get through a lot of things that I hated, because I always knew that they were serving a purpose, getting me closer to where I eventually wanted to be. I might not have liked most of the jobs I did in my early life, but because I recognised that they were getting me nearer to the dream of owning a farm, I could put up with them. It was what got me through the casual labouring jobs I did after leaving school at sixteen, with no qualifications. And it was what got me through a much worse experience, when I decided a year later to take one of the only other options open to someone like me back then, and joined the army. I don't know what I expected it to be like, but they certainly knew what to think of a mouthy black kid like me. I spent most of my time in trouble, being kicked around and having the shit knocked out of me both inside and outside the boxing ring.

I managed a year before being sent on my way with a dishonourable discharge. Now the army might have got rid of me, but I came out of the experience with my spirit intact. If you think about it, that is what the military are masters at: stripping people down and rebuilding them in the image of a soldier, with iron discipline and without many big or inconvenient ideas of their own. I took my beatings, but I never allowed them to break me; I had too strong a dream about what I wanted to achieve, and none of that involved square bashing or running up and down hills. That attitude may not have served me well as a trainee paratrooper, but it was essential in making me what I have since become. Because I had that dream, something to cling onto even when I was having to do work I hated and suffering all sorts of indignity, I had a place to go where no one could really hurt me, however hard they might kick or punch.

You might be in a similar situation yourself, perhaps stuck in a job or a career that you no longer enjoy or find fulfilling, feeling like every week is the same and that you are not really alive in your work. The first step to escaping that is to work out your dream: what you want to achieve. It must be something that you can throw your whole self into, an idea to believe in and commit to. All the studies tell us that religious observance is on the steady decline, but I don't think the essential truth has changed that people want something spiritual to believe in and guide them. They want something bigger than their everyday lives to provide meaning. A dream can provide that: it takes you beyond the mundane and into the realm of possibility. Of what might be. Of what you want to be. It gives you the focus to do something with your life and the optimism that you can achieve better, for yourself and your family. Above all, it gives you hope – something no one should live without, and which, when you are at the bottom of the pile, is really all you have to hold onto.

Of course, we all have dreams in our life, but too many of them are just idle thoughts, gentle daydreams about things we might like to do or try our hand at. The dreams I'm talking about are real, consuming passions. Something you will be motivated to pursue, and to keep trying even when it seems like there is no way to achieve it. Something that lights a fire within you. A real dream carries real jeopardy: the possibility that you might fail, and not only that, but that you might lose what you already have in the process. That is what makes it exciting; and that is what gives you the real necessity to do everything in your power to make it succeed. I have been living with my dream for almost five decades now; what I've learned in that time is that dreams are not static things, but ideas that you carry throughout your life and which evolve and change with you as a person. Bringing a dream to fulfilment is not a simple or swift matter. It takes time, commitment, perseverance and openness. In particular, I have learned that there are three things you need to have to shape and achieve your life's dream.

1) You need space

Your first reaction to reading this might well be that 'I'm too busy'. It's a common complaint in a world where we are all attached to mobile phones and constantly dealing with a deluge of communications – from work, family and friends. We are conditioned to think that the last thing to grab our attention is the most important one, and that we don't have time to concentrate on anything else.

In fact, the life dominated by technology can only ever be one that is lived in pure survival mode. We con ourselves that being efficient in answering emails is the same as actually getting things done; that holding meetings is progress; and that ticking things off a list equals success. It's the most logical way of making sense of a world dominated by technology, where the amount of information we have to handle is getting out of hand. It might be logical, but it's also nonsense. You can busy yourself in tasks and activity, but ask yourself this: what is it achieving and where is it taking you? It's quite possible to spend days, weeks and years consumed by activity that holds very little meaning. And that is because such work becomes an end in itself; it is self-perpetuating and unfulfilling. But it does fill the days and pay the bills.

If survival is enough, then that might be sufficient. But if you want to do things, to really achieve and to stand out, then you have to find ways of getting away from the everyday white noise and clutter. You have to carve out the space to dream. Space is so important because we all have an everyday life and existence that can easily fill our waking hours. If we become a slave to that routine, then that is all we will ever do. And the only way to get away from it, to break the cycle, is to make a concerted effort to give yourself space.

That space can be physical space, and I have talked about how my father's allotment was so important to me in providing a refuge from the poverty and overcrowding that surrounded me growing up. That was the everyday existence I wanted to escape, and that little oasis provided me with the space I needed to dream of how I might do it. You may have such a space of your own, a room or a garden you can retreat to. But it doesn't need to be a physical space. Ultimately, you can be in a prison cell and still find the space to dream. The real space you need is in the mind. Why? Because the limitations we face are so often those that we place upon ourselves. They are the lack of self-belief and the fear of trying something that might fail. They are the survival instinct, the voice that says you can't do this or you shouldn't do that. The one that sees jeopardy and wants to run a mile from it, back to the safety of the familiar comfort zone. Most people are their own worst enemies and their own biggest detractors. We get stuck in a job or lifestyle that we don't enjoy, because we lack the confidence to take a step outside it.

As someone who started life on society's dustbin heap, I can tell you that it is possible to achieve your dreams, whatever your circumstances. You don't have to be rich, privileged or with a ready network of people ready to give you a leg up. Only one thing can guarantee your failure to achieve something, and that is if you yourself discount the possibility. If you start with a negative mindset, then you may as well forget it. Whether that is casting doubt on your own abilities or bemoaning your circumstances and lack of opportunity, such negativity is the death knell for dreams and potential.

The very first thing you must do, if you want to change your life or do something new, is create the space to dream. Put aside your doubts and your preconceptions and just focus on the end goal. Think about the one thing you most want to achieve. It could be something you have imagined doing since childhood, or an ambition that has grown with your career: often that will be to leave the corporate herd and start something of your own. Whatever it is, give yourself the space to really focus on it, without putting all sorts of mental hurdles in your way about the difficulties you will face and reasons why your dream might not happen. Just think about it. About how it would feel and what it would mean to you. Start to dream about what it would be like to achieve it. And if that lights a fire in you, if that is something you know would change your life for the better, and you are prepared to embrace the risk and adversity needed to achieve it, then you are getting somewhere. Without that space to dream and to imagine, it is all too easy to get sucked into the routine and the reality of your everyday existence, and to never get close to escaping it.

I can tell you from experience that it is bloody hard to break out of that, to get beyond the expectations people have for you and to do something that is really unusual and against the grain. It takes a hell of a lot more than just having a big dream, but don't try it without one. And don't expect to find that dream unless you create the space for it to emerge, to grow and become compelling enough to pursue.

2) You need time

Space is what can help you to nurture and build your dream, but to achieve it will take time. In today's world we have become rather hooked on instant satisfaction, on finding things out or having them delivered at the touch of a button. But it remains true that if you want to achieve something that is meaningful and lasting in your life, you will need time. Things that matter aren't built overnight and you will need the great virtue of patience if you are to succeed in making your dream a reality.

There is a mindset that you need when pursuing a big dream, to start a business, write a novel or build a new life in another country. That is about accepting that it is a journey that may have many different stages to it. It might not be a straightforward road that you can simply cruise down; in fact, is is very unlikely to be that straightforward! More often, it will be a long and winding road that takes you to places you don't expect and to others that seem very unpromising. You might do jobs that you don't enjoy or that don't seem directly relevant to your dream. That doesn't have to matter, as long as these things are serving a greater purpose, moving you in some way towards what it is that you really want. There is a difference between doing rubbish jobs when you have no dream in mind, and taking them on when you do. If you have that focus, and if you know that this is just something that is helping to give you the platform and the money to do what you really want, then that is worthwhile.

After getting kicked out of the army, I worked in catering for quite a few years. It was about the only qualification I could hope to get, and so I knuckled down and worked in kitchens, some distinguished and others much less so. I knew it wasn't what I wanted to do with my life, but it gave me some experience in working with food, and allowed me to support myself. The reality is that you won't always be able to get the life or job you want in one big leap. You have to be realistic about the gap between where you are now and where you want to be in the future. And that may mean accepting some things you don't want to do, if they help you get closer to the thing you do want.

Think of an athlete training for the Olympics. They don't just turn up to a race. Behind a few minutes of high-level performance are months and years of training in preparation for the big moment. You will also need to train to achieve your dreams; you need to be prepared to put in the long hours, whether it's getting better at a specific skill, or just getting yourself into a position where you are ready to go for it.

While you are slogging away and working to get yourself in reach of your dream, the important thing is that you never lose sight of it. Elite athletes are defined by their focus on the end goal: the personal best, the big race or match. You need to be similarly ruthless in your focus, to avoid letting what should be your training become a comfort zone of its own. I could have had a perfectly decent life as a chef, but I was always restless because I had made the promise to myself that I would one day own the farm, and that was on my conscience as something I had to achieve.

Because dreams are hard to achieve and because they take time, it is easy to find them eroded by the experience of having to survive. You will have plenty of ups and downs, moments when what you are working towards seems impossible. And that is the most important training of all. Your dream is going to take a battering from your own experiences, from the people who question and deride it, and from the sheer time it takes to properly achieve. And if it can survive that, then it can most likely be achieved, however long it takes.

3) You need to talk

No one can achieve their dream single-handedly. If you want to turn your burning passion into something real, you will need to enlist the support of other people: the guardian angels we all need to succeed in life and achieve our dreams. And you can't get people's help if you don't tell them what you are trying to do. To have any hope of achieving your dream, you have to get used to talking about it.

That is harder than it sounds, when dreams are so personal and fragile. We build a picture in our heads about who we want to be and what we most desire to achieve. In the safe space of our own minds, those hazy notions can start to become powerful dreams, protected from the judgement and criticism of other people. But a dream cannot succeed if it stays forever in your own head. However difficult it might seem, there will come a time when you have to let it out of the protective cocoon, to expose your ambition to the harsh realities of the real world.

Talking about your innermost thoughts and ambitions takes a good deal of courage: as a young man, I knew that my dream of owning a farm would be laughed at by my family and classmates in inner-city Birmingham. It wasn't until my late teens that I actually started giving voice to that dream. We all have to conquer that sense of self-doubt and self-consciousness that comes with speaking up about something that isn't real, sounds ambitious and might come across as fanciful or idealistic.

Once you have started to talk about your dream, get ready for the brickbats to start flying your way. The first people I started to tell were my parents. They didn't just think it was a stupid idea, I think they were actually insulted by it. For me to be sticking my head above the parapet in that way, trying to do something completely outside their frame of reference, was more than foolhardy in their view. It was downright stupidity and arrogance that would harm my ability to get the safe, steady job that they thought I should aspire to.

There are many reasons why people will criticise your dreams and try to stop you from pursuing them. Some, like my parents, are fundamentally motivated by their concern for you. They want you to avoid jeopardy and to follow the safer road. Others, more typically friends and colleagues, are more likely to be motivated by how your ambitions make them feel about themselves. If they feel stuck themselves in the job you share, they might feel jealous that someone is making a break for it, and frustrated by their own inability or unwillingness to do the same. That was the response I got when I was working in catering and would regularly shout the odds about how I wasn't going to be stuck in this crappy job in a decade's time. By putting yourself out there, by saying you want to do something different and better, you are also putting a target on your back for people who don't want to see their friends and peers rise above their own level. The jeopardy of having a big, overtly unrealistic dream, is that you may be the only one who actually believes in it, and it gives other people a stick to beat you with.

You have to remember that people won't see your dreams as merely a reflection on you, but also on them. We all judge our own lives in part by the success of our friends, people we grew up with and others of the same age. Our competitive instinct kicks in when we see people around us starting to succeed, so by talking about your dream to your friends, family and colleagues, you are kicking a potential hornet's nest of other people's own self-esteem and ambitions. In my own case, I faced a lot of resentment for trying to break the mould of what was expected for someone like me. My peers thought that I wasn't just off my rocker, but actively giving up on the struggle that the black community was engaged in at that time; trying to escape those realities rather than taking my punishment and suffering in solidarity.

What I was doing was setting out my stall as an outsider, saying that I didn't want to belong to the club that would have me, but to be someone who lived by my own rules. It is much easier to belong than to be someone who is truly independent. When you set out with a big dream, remember that you are not just moving towards something new, but leaving behind something old. Don't be surprised if the people you are leaving behind try to stop you, or resent you for what you are trying to do. That is all part of the jeopardy of being an outsider, setting your own path and following a big dream.

All these are some of the difficulties you will face when you start to talk about your dream. This is the moment when it starts to get real. Without doubt, talking about your dreams is a difficult thing to do, both in terms of plucking up the courage in the first place and then dealing with what the people you tell will throw back at you. Yet, however hard it might be, starting to talk about your big ambition is one of the most important steps on the road to achieving it. For you, it is the beginning of taking the idea out of your imagination and towards reality: when you have to put it into words or writing, there is something tangible that didn't exist before, and that is important. Even more importantly, once the dream is out there, people know about it and can help you. Not everyone will be looking to hold you back or chip away at your ambitions. There will be others who believe in you and help you on your way; you may not know yet who they are, and quite possibly you have not yet even met them. But you never know when someone completely unexpected might be able to give you the opportunity that really makes the difference. And none of that can happen unless you get out there and start talking about your big dream.

* * *

A dream, then, is where your journey towards a life lived with jeopardy begins. We can all have idle thoughts: there is no risk connected with them when they remain locked in our heads, and we do not act on them. It is when you first start to express your dream, to share and talk about it, that you discover it is not so easy. People criticise your vision and may even laugh at you. Your first baby steps may get you nowhere. From thinking about what it would be like to fulfil the dream, you are suddenly faced with the reality of what it will take to get there; how far you still have to go and how perilous the road ahead appears.

That is good. It may not feel like it, but if you are feeling that pain and difficulty – worried about what it will take, and unsure about whether you can succeed – then you have done something vitally important. You have stepped outside the realm of survival and into the land of jeopardy. You have given yourself a purpose and a focus. And you are in a place where you will make mistakes, learn from them, and get better with every day. It is the dream, the all-powerful vision for what we want to make of ourselves and our lives, that makes those first steps possible. Dreams are your starting point and they become a reference point you return to when times are tough and you're not sure what to do next.

A dream is needed because not everything you do on the road to achieving it will seem worthwhile. There wasn't much glamour for me in my twenties, washing pots and microwaving burgers in restaurant kitchens, but because I had the dream I could put up with it. I knew that all this nonsense work was, in its own small way, contributing to what I really wanted, taking me a few small steps further towards my goal.

So if you are someone who thinks that you haven't got the time to waste on dreams, then I would say this to you. It's actually the other way around: you can't afford not to have a dream, a burning ambition for your life, if you want to escape your comfort zone and really achieve things. Many of us are hard-wired to be what we call pragmatic and to disdain dreams as frivolous and distracting. This is one of the most significant mental hurdles you will have to overcome: your in-built instincts to play it safe and avoid the potential for failure and criticism. You need to overcome your own misgivings and those of others. People say they can't dream, but they can. They say they haven't got any choices, but they do. And they say there isn't time, but there is.

A dream is a necessity, not a nice-to-have. It is the anchor for everything you still want to do. Your idea might seem stupid, outlandish or unachievable when you first start to think about it, but there is nothing wrong with aiming high. In fact, you need to do just that, to dream of something beyond what you immediately know you are capable of, to set targets that are going to stress and stretch you, and to commit to doing things you have never tried before. For if you do that, you are truly accepting jeopardy into your life, and once you have, then things can really start to happen.

CHAPTER 4

Make a friend of fear

With a dream, you have one of the most important tools you will need to succeed in life. You have taken a crucial first step towards a life lived with jeopardy. But many more people have big dreams than ever achieve them. Many never even take that first step towards trying. There are numerous reasons for this, but there is one thing above all that holds people back. That is fear.

Fear is so often what stops people from changing their lives and achieving their dreams. It is the hidden force that suppresses self-belief and thwarts ambition. Whether we realise it or not, most of our lives are ruled by fear. We are afraid of everything going wrong, losing our job and ending up on the scrapheap. We fear getting ill or losing the people we love. We fear the things we can't do, and that others will find out about our shortcomings. And we fear things that shouldn't really matter at all: getting something wrong, being embarrassed in front of our friends or colleagues, looking stupid.

Fear is ingrained in our DNA, as a species and as

individuals. And it is intrinsic to any life lived with jeopardy, because you will encounter it more often, and need to learn better how to cope with it. If you revert to the natural instinct to shy away from fear, it will stop you from focusing on the things that really matter. Every day you spend trying to offset something you are afraid of is one that you are not putting towards achieving your dream. You become a prisoner of fear.

Of course, fear exists for a good reason. It's what stops us putting our hand in a fire, or crossing the road without checking if we are about to be run over. And many people have very real reasons to be afraid, be they personal, financial or political. But there is another kind of fear, an unspoken one that affects people who do not generally go about their daily lives feeling afraid. This is the fear that, somehow, what we have is about to be taken away from us. That we are about to be unmasked as a fraud. That we aren't good enough to achieve the things we really want.

You can see this fear all around you, in people who are stuck in jobs and lifestyles they don't enjoy. And in companies, especially big corporations, where entire cultures are based on damage limitation, arse-covering and an obsessive aversion to taking responsibility. People will go to extraordinary lengths to avoid being blamed for things, to the point where they hardly dare do anything at all. That is fear: the great fuel for the survivor's mentality. It is the rejection of jeopardy and it prevents people from seeking opportunities for a better life and a more interesting career. Fear is what keeps people staying put, in the life, job or relationship they already have, whether they like it or not.

That is the kind of fear that you must recognise and address in your own life, if you want to to start doing the things that really matter to you. What are the things you are afraid of? What do you worry about and where do you doubt yourself? You have to be honest with yourself before you can start dealing with the things that make you afraid and get beyond the barriers you unknowingly place in your way.

The simple fact is that we all have fear in our lives. Even the most powerful CEO, the top-achieving athlete and the most virtuoso musician is afraid of something, often far more than you would ever imagine from the outside. The question is, how can you stop fear from inhibiting your ability to get what you want in life and to achieve your dream? How do you start embracing the jeopardy of being just afraid enough to achieve something meaningful, rather than being too scared to even have a go in the first place?

I have been afraid for most of my life. Like many people who grew up in poverty, I had an unstable childhood, one constantly oppressed by the feeling that some great disaster was waiting around the corner. In that situation you are living with permanent uncertainty, afraid that there won't be enough food or money to go around. There are only two ways to respond: either you use it as a motivator, becoming the person who works the hardest and does everything in their power to get out of the circumstances that life has put you in; or you get engulfed by that fear and let it control you and dominate your life.

This is one of the great choices we will all face. Do we make fear our friend or let it become our enemy? As a friend, fear can be one of the most powerful forces to motivate us and drive us forward. To be successful, you need a little fear to create the necessity to keep going, to break down obstacles and to overcome adversity. Fear puts us on our mettle: it sharpens focus, makes the mind work quicker, forces us to make decisions that we might otherwise put off into the land of never-never. In too great a quantity, however, fear becomes your enemy: a source of negative energy, clouding your judgement and inhibiting your willingness to take risks.

We all have to accept that we will live with fear: it is not a dragon that can be slain once and for all, but a constant companion that will be with you whatever you do and wherever you go, influencing how you think and second-guessing what you decide. Our fears reflect our lives, both past and future. To manage them, we have to understand where they come from and what they represent.

I have had fear as both friend and enemy at different points in my life. For me, it is one of the most interesting and important ingredients in success: how we understand and cope with it, whether we are empowered or under-mined by it. In this chapter, I look at fear in all its forms: the different things we are afraid of, the different sources of fear, and how you can take a logical approach to cope with irrational feelings, managing your fear to make sure that it doesn't end up managing you.

Fear of the known

The most obvious source of fear in our lives is experience. We are once bitten, twice shy – afraid of things that went wrong the first or last time we tried them. A child who falls off their bike badly will generally be wary of getting back onto it. Even as adults, we sometimes keep away from the foods that we learned to dislike in our early years. We fear things that we know we don't like, or that might put us in harm's way.

These known fears can be small things that have little impact on our lives; but they can also be very significant ones that determine our ability to succeed. Because I grew up in poverty, and know what it is like to not have food on the table, I have always been driven by an essential motivation never to go back to that place. The fear of being back where you started, and having everything you have worked for taken away from you, becomes all-consuming. And out of that fear comes motivation. Having worked so hard to escape, I was never going to ease up and risk losing what I had earned. At the BBC, surrounded by people from comfortable backgrounds and good schools, I worked twice as hard to make sure that I wouldn't be chucked out, or shown up as the fraud that I often worried I was.

Really, because you know what the alternative looks like, you give yourself no option but to succeed. It is no coincidence that many successful, self-made people come from backgrounds like mine. When you do, the fear of being made to go back, and the passion to build a better life for yourself and your children, is so overwhelming that it keeps you going no matter what. That has been my story and it is the same with many people I have worked with. Gordon Ramsay, whose television career I helped start in the 1990s, is another good example. He had a difficult childhood: his father was abusive, and by the age of sixteen he had lived in seventeen different homes. When I knew him, you could see how driven he was, obsessed with doing well because the alternative did not bear thinking about.

People like Gordon are a classic example of making fear your friend, turning what you are afraid of into a powerful source of motivation. This fear of the known is something you can harness and use to your advantage. I knew I could never go back to the life I had been born into, and that is the strongest incentive you can ever have. It is the same if you have been in a job you hated, or a relationship that went wrong. You know you never want to repeat the experience, and it gives you the focus and determination to do better. You can find all the motivation you need in the things that you have been through and never want to do again. That is the fire in the belly that we all need to grab hold of our dreams.

Fear of the unknown

As much as we fear the things we know, we are often even more afraid of those we don't know. Fear of the unknown, the untried and the untested, is one of the greatest barriers to success in all our lives. Whether we like it or not, most of us build some sort of comfort zone in our personal and professional lives: a space where we know the people, follow a routine and do work that we can do well, with ease. It is quite possible to live your life like that, happily and blamelessly, but it is not possible to achieve great things. Dreams are not fulfilled from a place of safety. They can only be pursued through voyaging into new territory, embracing the jeopardy of the unknown.

To do anything really meaningful in life, you will have to meet people, do things and put yourself in situations that are alien to what you know and are comfortable with. You have to test yourself in arenas where you can't be sure that you will succeed. And you will be afraid of trying. That is completely natural. When doing anything for the first time it is very unlikely that you will have all the skills or knowledge you will need to succeed. Why should you? But those are things you can pick up along the way if you have the determination, passion and luck to eventually succeed. The far greater challenge is plucking up the courage to have a go in the first place, to be brave enough to take that first step into the unknown.

For many people, their fear of the unknown becomes an enemy, a barrier to progress that stops them getting started in the first place. Having a dream is one thing, but the courage to actually pursue it is something else entirely.

How, then, can you make fear of the unknown your friend? The most important thing is to accept that failure is possible, even likely, and to understand that this does not matter nearly as much as you think. We have a very strange culture around failure, where it is seen as shameful and something to be avoided at all costs. In fact, there is a great deal of learning to be gained when you try things that don't work. In business, many successful entrepreneurs will be those who are on their second or third business, benefiting from what the first failed ventures taught them. It is a myth that you can go through life without collecting some battle scars along the way; in the long run, you will be much better for them. And while you can live a life that is shielded in many ways from failure, it will not be as fulfilling as one in which you embrace the possibility of losing and learn from your mistakes. Don't let the fear of failure get in the way of stepping into the unknown.

You also need to see that there is a fine line between harnessing fear, making it your friend, and letting it engulf you. Think of it as a powerful drug or medicine: in moderation, it can have significant benefits, but take too much and you will feel the side-effects pretty quickly. A little bit of fear makes us alert, it gets the adrenaline pumping and helps the survival instinct to kick in. Too much and we just want to run from the fight, find shelter and never come out again. Then fear is no longer motivating us, but inhibiting us, providing a million reasons why we can't do something, or shouldn't.

The important thing is to get the dose right: if you are absolutely terrified of something, you should listen to that instinct. There is no point taking a big step into the unknown if you have no confidence in your ability to succeed. But if the thing you are thinking about makes you just a little afraid, gives you butterflies in your stomach and makes you doubt that you are good enough, then you should back yourself. That means you are pushing your limits, without going miles beyond them. You are leaving your comfort zone and giving yourself the best chance to really succeed. And you will need that jeopardy if you are ever going to come close to achieving your dreams.

Fear of ourselves

Taking that step into the unknown is one of the most important things you can do. But even when that frontier has been crossed, there is a fear that never goes away, and that is about ourselves. Are we really good enough? Do we have what it takes? Will we be shown up as a fraud in front of our friends and colleagues?

I spent much of my life afraid, not just of having to go back to the poverty I had been born into, but of revealing a secret that I thought could cost me everything. This was my dyslexia. Remember, I was at school in the 1960s, when the condition was not at all understood and people like me were written off as thick. I had teachers telling me that I would never amount to anything, and I left school without a single qualification. If I had been happy to pursue the life laid out for me, in labouring and low-skilled jobs, that would not have been a problem. But when I got my break at the BBC, I was suddenly surrounded by people who were very highly educated and who had all sorts of capabilities I did not.

For instance, a one-minute script that a colleague would have dashed off in an hour or less would take me all day. But I was so afraid of being unmasked that I would work through the nights, labouring over every word and never asking for help. I was completely terrified that if I talked about the difficulties I was having, I would be thrown out of my precious job and back onto the dustbin heap. Having worked so hard to get my foot in the door, I wasn't about to give anyone the chance to slam it in my face. So I lived in fear and had to work like a maniac as a result.

Today I see my dyslexia as one of the most important things about me as a person, and as an entrepreneur. Those of us who are dyslexic may not be able to win the spelling bee, but we have a creativity that is often much more powerful and uninhibited. It can be a huge advantage when you are dealing with problems in business or trying to create something new. Very slowly, we are getting to a place in our society where people whose brains work differently are appreciated for who they are, and for the unique perspective they can offer. While dyslexics once lived in fear of being branded stupid and useless, today we can make something positive of our difference.

I believe that this attitude is one we all need in order to manage the fears that we all have about ourselves, our abilities and our self-worth. We fear the things we cannot do (or think we can't), focusing obsessively on these shortcomings, rather than looking at the things we can do well instead. We follow our instincts to recoil from the things we fear rather than engaging with them and seeing opportunities that may exist to make a virtue of them. Something you think of as a weakness might actually give you a competitive advantage: to see the world a different way, have greater empathy, or appreciation for other people. As a dyslexic, I have one of the most valuable perspectives a person can have, which is that of the outsider. In business, when there is a premium on seeing things differently and presenting new solutions to old problems, that is one of the most valuable things you can have.

The fear I once had of my dyslexia was the fear that we all have about making ourselves vulnerable. We all have our vulnerabilities, our weak spots, the things we don't want others to see or know. And we expend a huge amount of energy trying to conceal these, so that no one will ever find out about them and take advantage. Whereas, in fact, vulnerability is hugely important and something that should be primarily seen as positive; it is the place from where all creativity and innovation emerge. Only by making ourselves vulnerable – by taking risks, being honest about ourselves and other people, and putting our reputation on the line – can we get the things we want. Vulnerability is one of the most powerful tools we have, and it has been one of the defining features of my life. It is also one of the things people are most afraid of, but we must learn instead to embrace it.

Not all fears can be conquered, but they can be managed, and when it comes to fears about ourselves, we have to be more open-minded about our strengths and weaknesses, and more welcoming of our vulnerabilities. Don't make assumptions about what you are and aren't good at, or what other people will think about you. And don't let the fear of what you think you can't do inhibit you from taking steps towards pursuing your dream.

Fear of others

The fear we feel naturally as humans is not the only kind that you will encounter. There is another fear, one that we do not generate ourselves, but which is actively promoted by other people. Anyone who has tried to start a business will have met them: the fearmongers who will whisper in your ear about the possibility of failure; those who will gaze out onto the horizon of your dream and point out all the places where you could trip and fall. The reality is that anyone who tries to do something ambitious, unusual or risky will face fearmongers who try to stop them. One of the biggest obstacles to embracing jeopardy is not just your own fear, but the fear promoted by those people who will try and hold you back.

If you are going to pursue a big dream, you have to see and understand fearmongers for what they are. Not all have bad intentions: some will be friends or family who are trying to protect you from harm. That is what I experienced with my own parents, who tried to steer me away from the dream of becoming a farmer towards aspirations they understood better. Others have less admirable motives: they don't want to see a colleague or peer succeed where they could not. These kinds of fearmongers are widespread in the corporate world, where so many people are focused not on achieving results for their employer, but on securing their own position within the hierarchy. You will find people whose entire career existence is dedicated to maintaining the status quo and avoiding change that could affect their precious positions. When I ran a marketing agency working with food and drink brands, I had the constant frustration of dealing with people whose only response to a new idea would be to second-guess what their boss would think of it. In that environment, it is almost impossible to get good work done.

These are people who are themselves afraid, and who look to protect themselves by franchising fear. Still more are looking to make money as fearmongers: these are the industries, from law to accountancy, that profit hugely off getting people to fear what might go wrong, and to pay them as insurance against it. In the early days of running a business, you will be inundated with these people, trying to make you afraid of things that might happen: you could get sued by an employee, you could get hacked, you could suffer a manufacturing failure and be left with defective products. These are the possible futures which fearmongers use to scare people into giving them money. That is not to say that we don't need lawyers, accountants or insurers. They have their place, but you also have to recognise that if entrepreneurs did everything these people told them, their businesses would never get off the ground. By contrast, fearmongers are people who don't take risks themselves, but who make money off those who do.

For fearmongers, the moment of greatest opportunity arrives when something goes wrong. Aha, they will say to you, I told you that was a bad idea. Didn't we say this would never work? When mishaps occur, fearmongers move in to try and seize control, to squeeze out risk and throw out innovation. I have seen this happen often in the food business, with small suppliers tossed onto the fire in favour

of 'safer' big companies by everyone from retailers to manufacturers, often after something had gone wrong. It's not
worth the hassle, they say. It's just too big a risk. Yet that
in itself is a risky proposition, because it assumes that the
landscape today is never going to change. It assumes that
big suppliers will always remain successful, and that small
ones will never grow. It gives you a guarantee for the short
term, but no insurance against the change that the future
will bring. Fearmongers can sometimes help you analyse
what is right in front of you, right now, but they cannot
make you resilient for a world of change. Their advice can
be as risky as the things they warn you off doing.

In the end, very little that is good in life or business
comes without risk, and that is not something that can
be endlessly hedged or litigated. Just as you have to look
logically at your own fears, you need to be rational with
the fearmongers: separating the good advice from the scare
stories. You need to see people like this for who they are,
with all their limitations, because otherwise you will let the
drip, drip of their negativity diminish your ambition and
erode your self-belief. Don't let the fear that other people
manufacture be the thing that stops you from pursuing
your dreams. Embracing jeopardy means you will have to
take risks and make decisions that others would not. And
you need to be guided by your own instincts and tolerance
for fear, not those of other people.

Fear of the future

So much of what we fear in life is about the future. What will happen to us tomorrow, next week, next year? What will happen if we leave our jobs, or pursue our dreams to start our business or move abroad? What will happen if we confess our love to someone when we don't know what they will say in return? What will happen if we put our trust in someone we don't yet fully know?

'What if?' can be the mentality of the dreamer: looking forward towards the opportunity and potential of new ideas, people and circumstances. But more often it will be a space in which we allow our fears to grow. Onto an uncertain future, we project all sorts of disaster that might befall us, in a world that has moved beyond our control.

It is easy to see the world as an obstacle course just waiting to trip you up, focusing only on the things that might go wrong in your life. The problem with this mind-set is that your whole existence becomes ruled by fear. Everything is seen through the lens of what you might lose, or disasters that might befall you. Some people think that this is a rational way to live, because by anticipating what might happen, you can do more to protect yourself against it. This is one of the great fallacies. However much we try to predict what will happen tomorrow and protect ourselves against it, the fact is that we can't. Bad things are going to happen. You will suffer adversity and hurt. And we are all going to die. Anyone who tries to live in denial of those facts is simply wasting energy on controlling what cannot be controlled. It is a dangerous illusion that distracts people from focusing their efforts on the things that really matter: rather than working hard to move forward, you are expending energy on just standing still.

The most damaging thing about this endemic fear of the future is that it stops people from living for today. We put off the important decisions, the things we are worried about, or the things we want to do until that mythical world of tomorrow, in which the consequences can't touch us. But then one tomorrow becomes another and, before you know it, the opportunity to do that thing has passed you by. There is a jeopardy in making big decisions today, because then we have to live with the consequences here and now, but unless you grasp that the things you want in life will generally elude you.

The greatest cure for a fear of all the bad things that might occur in the future is having one of those things actually happen to you. In my late fifties, I was struck down by an acute form of leukaemia. The complications of that, and the stem-cell transplant that helped treat me, left me in hospital for an entire year. The initial prognosis was very bad, and it was clear that my chances of survival were relatively slim. When you get ill, the fear of the future becomes very real. You face your own mortality, and you think about what your death would mean for your family and the people around you.

It is a terrifying experience, but there is one hidden benefit to serious illness – and that is the clarity it brings. Staring death in the face has the magical effect of clearing all of life's clutter away. Suddenly, everything that had seemed so important yesterday – little things in your business or personal life – ceases to matter. The junk is cleared to one side, and you focus on what really matters: your family, your life's work, the legacy you want to leave. After I made it through the illness and got out of hospital, that clarity stayed with me. I am now more focused than ever on what I want to achieve in my life, and am more efficient in how I go about doing it.

I am certainly not recommending that you seek a near-death experience! But my lesson from that period in my life was that, even as someone who thought of themselves as a very focused and driven entrepreneur, I had far too much clutter and distraction in my life. Too many little fears about the future were getting in the way of what really mattered. We all have them, and they are one of the easiest types of fear to deal with. That is because they are not real: not based on real experience or real fear about serious things that can go wrong. Our fears about the future are so often just displacement activity or procrastination, because the thing we really fear is doing something where we cannot know or control the result.

What I always say to people is that you should conduct an annual audit – of things on your mind and everything you are worrying about. Have a mental spring clean and think hard about where you are wasting your effort when it could be better spent on things you actually want to achieve. Focus is one of the most precious things you can have in life, and fear is one of the primary forces that can deprive you of it. When you start putting your full time and energy towards your dream, you will be amazed at what you can achieve.

* * *

Fear is something we will encounter in many different forms: there are the fears that grow within us, the ones other people try to impose upon us, and fears of everything from being returned to a past we escaped from, to being propelled into an unknown future. In all cases, the one thing we have to accept is that fear will always be with us, and no significant endeavour will ever come without sparking new fears or reigniting old ones.

We cannot control when fear will strike us, but we can control our response to it. Often you will hear people talk about conquering fear, as if it is a hurdle that can be jumped once and will never be encountered again. I prefer to think about *managing* fear: understanding how it affects us and taking a rational approach to often deeply irrational emotions. We cannot ever finally conquer fear and that is a good thing, because we need it: just enough to keep our instincts sharp and stop us from getting complacent. In the right dose, fear is an asset and it is a signal that we are doing the right things, pushing beyond our comfort zone.

So you need to manage fear, to make it your friend and ensure that it is helping you move forward, rather than tying you up in knots of indecision. There are many different ways to do this, but they all come down to being logical and not getting caught up in the emotions of what you are afraid of. You need to rule over your fears, not ride the rollercoaster with them. If you fear failure, think whether it would actually be that bad, or whether you might actually learn something. If you fear something you cannot do, look at ways of either mitigating that or emphasising a different strength that you have. If you fear something you do not know, try a small dose of it to inoculate yourself against that anxiety. And if you are afraid because of someone else's warnings, ask yourself why they are doing that, what their motive is and how reliable a witness they really are.

Learn to recognise fear and to get comfortable with it, for it is one of the signs that you are starting to live with jeopardy, to push the limits of your ability and to put yourself in the position to achieve things. No dream can be pursued without jeopardy, and managing fear is one of the main skills you will have to learn on that journey. With fear it is a simple equation: either fear is controlling you, or you are controlling it. Once you are understanding, embracing and assessing your fears – treating them in the most rational and objective way possible – then you are in charge, and that alone is half the battle.

CHAPTER 5

Be unprofessionally passionate

'I am the Black Farmer, and this is my soul.' Those were the closing words of our first television advert, which aired a full decade after I started the business. We had waited a long time and I didn't want another conventional food and drink advert. Working with Tony Kaye, the director of *American History X*, we created something that no one else could have: a madcap slice of rural Britain, complete with fields, forests, flags and Morris dancers. There were no pack shots, no mention of our key selling points, and just one glimpse of our brand.

Instead, what I wanted the advert to convey was the fundamental passions that have driven The Black Farmer since day one: a love for rural Britain, for farming and the outdoors. A passion for real produce and the care and skill that goes into making great food. These were things that motivated me long before I knew my business would sell sausages.

Mine is a business that has always been about the real passions that motivate me in life; it is a vehicle to share and celebrate them with the world. In building it I have learned one of my most important lessons: that passion – which we all have somewhere, deep down, but are often encouraged to suppress or hide away – is actually one of the essential assets for building a business or a career.

Let us be honest. At first glance, a sausage is not the most exciting thing to be selling. How interesting can you really make some off-cuts of meat and water compressed into a bit of animal intestine? The answer is, you can only make it interesting if you are passionate about it. You need to show that you have real reasons to be doing this, a motivation that is about more than making money from sausage meat.

With The Black Farmer that is exactly what we did. As a brand it has always been about selling who I am and what I believe in, as much as it is premium fresh produce. The whole name and brand is about telling my unusual story, catching eyes and raising eyebrows. It is not just about an arresting first impression, but expressing my passion for farming and the British countryside, and revelling in my outsider status. A black farmer in Cornwall: no one else could nick or rip off that idea. It is a challenge to people's assumptions about farming and who farmers are, and something that creates jeopardy in the mind of the consumer, because they do not know exactly what they should be thinking. Above all, the brand is a fundamental expression of passion: one that immediately elevates our proposition beyond the mere facts of the produce we are selling.

The Black Farmer is a business that began with my childhood dream to own a farm, and it has grown through my passion to be a pathfinder for black Britons into a rural world, where traditionally we have had no place. When you have that passion and are willing to share it, you give people something to understand beyond a logo or words on a packet. There is an idea to buy into, as well as a product to purchase. When you are trying to connect with customers, it is not enough to have a great product; of course, I think our sausages are the best on the market, and we have worked hard to differentiate ourselves through great ingredients, and factors such as being the first gluten-free sausage on the market. But ultimately, quality can only be your baseline. You need something more, an emotional connection with the people who you are selling to. People might buy once on price, but they will return for a brand they can really empathise with. And then you have real loyalty, which you can't build a business without.

It should be easy for us to harness passion in our working lives, and it should be something that we all look to make the most of. You might meet many people who have equivalent, or even better, skills than you – people who can think more quickly, and sell better and argue more persuasively. But if you are doing something that matters to you, something that you are passionate about, then you have the ability to make up for any and all shortfalls you may face, or imagine that you do. Passion can be the great leveller, giving you the strength and resolve to compete in any field, regardless of your qualifications or background. If you care more than the competition, then you are in with a chance, whatever advantages they may appear to have.

But if only it were that simple. While passion has the

potential to be one of our greatest weapons, there is real jeopardy in wielding it. The fact is, it makes a lot of people uncomfortable. Passion is often misinterpreted (sometimes wilfully) as anything from naive enthusiasm to unhelpful dissent or even aggression. People who show passion can be sidelined as too emotional and too instinct driven to make sensible decisions. It won't surprise you to learn that I think this is the height of nonsense, and that attempts to downplay passion are usually led by people who don't have any of their own, who are trying to shut down something that feels alien and threatening to them.

Passion is an easy thing to try and demean or discredit. It costs a person nothing to point the finger and start picking holes right, left and centre in someone's new idea. It's an easy way to look good from a place of safety, without risking any criticism or having to do any real work yourself. That is the reality that you must face if you are going to be someone with passion, whether you are working in someone else's business or running your own. There will always be people who try and use it against you, to undermine and trip you up. Some will genuinely feel threatened; others will think they are just being the reasonable ones. The fact is, passion provokes strong reactions and that is something you have to be prepared for.

The prize of passion, however, is much greater than the cost of those who will try and stand in your way. Because passion provides both the motivation and the toolkit to succeed. It gets you up in the morning and helps you keep going through good times and bad. It's also a compass for making progress in your career or business, and for working out the tough decisions. As an example, I talk in this chapter about how one of the most important business decisions I ever made, naming my company, was made by letting passion override the logic of what market researchers were telling me.

Passion is representative of your truest self, the things you really want and know deep down to be right. It is something you must never lose touch with if you want to unlock your full potential in life. It won't always make your life easy, and it will set some people against you, but if you want to escape survival mode then you need to harness passion, and to embrace the jeopardy of being someone who is sometimes prepared to defy what logic and consensus are telling them to do.

Defying logic

At a conference some years ago, I gave a talk about the importance of passion in my life and how it had driven me to achieve the things I have. When I came off the stage, I was stunned by the response of one fellow speaker, a high-profile UK entrepreneur. She said straight out that she didn't agree, and that in her view passion was overrated as an ingredient for success in business.

For me, that was flabbergasting, because if you have entrepreneurs saying that passion doesn't matter so much, then we are in trouble. In my experience, passion is the one thing, above all, that entrepreneurs have with which to distinguish themselves from the crowd. Remember that, to start a business, you are saying that you can do something better than the countless other companies that already do it. You are saying that you, on your own or with a small founding team, can compete with well-established, well-funded organisations with hundreds or thousands of people at their beck and call. You are saying that a brand nobody has ever heard of can gain traction in a market dominated by names with years, decades or even centuries of history.

If you were to run that all through the computer, it would tell you to shut up and go home. No purely rational critic would give you a chance. The point is, there often isn't a logical basis to a major undertaking, whether that is to start a business, turn your life upside down or enter a new relationship. You can't build an entirely rational justi-fication for something that doesn't yet exist, and you won't convince everyone (sometimes anyone) that it is likely to work. All you have is your passion, your belief and your commitment to make it work, to prove yourself right and others wrong. To make real this idea that so far exists only in your head.

This is why passion is so important, because it allows us to have big dreams, to look beyond what the evidence wants to tell us, and to defy the conventions that society seeks to place upon us. Without passion, people like my parents would never have left their homeland to try and find a better life in a strange country, where they knew nobody and precious little about the society they were about to become a part of. Without passion, someone like me would never have burned to get out of the poverty trap into which I was born, and to fulfil my lifetime dream of owning a farm. And an entrepreneur like Steve Jobs would never have fought like hell to build a company that could put computing power into the hands of the masses. It is passion that drives these dreams, big or small, individual or collective, creating the impetus that makes them possible. Without passion, we would all be stuck in the place we were born, living the lives our parents lived and never glimpsing the possibility that things could be different, that life could be better. For society and the individual, passion provides the pathway to progress; that is how it has always been. Without it, we would all still be living in caves.

In his famous Apple advert, Jobs talked about the 'crazy ones' who change the world: 'the misfits, the rebels, the ones who see things differently'. For me that is a fundamental expression of the power of passion, of people trying to do things that defy convention. It's important to remember that such gambits will often fail. But when they do succeed, their impact can be profound. And without passion, no one would even be having a go in the first place.

If you are trying to do something that completely defies the odds, then a cautious, evidence-based approach is no good to you. If you are doing something with real jeopardy, which carries the possibility of total failure, then the facts are never going to line up on your side, and you can't rely on them to make your case. A big dream will defy logic and reason; it won't be something that fits neatly into other people's worldview, and it won't be easy to get people to back you. That is where passion comes into play. When you are trying to do something that has never been done before, or breaking from the current state of play in a major way, you are often completely alone. You are the madman who is making a case to change something that other people think is working just fine, a lone voice that will have lots of people crossing the road to avoid you. Without lots of supporters, a track record or a mound of evidence behind you, all you really have is your passion. If you are pursuing a bold idea and a big dream, passion is often the one tool you will have in your kit: the one thing with which you can persuade people, drum up support and start to build what is in your head. It might not make sense to anyone else, but if you have that passion, then you have a chance.

That passion is what separates us from the machines and algorithms. It is what allows us to dream and do things that defy logic and reason, but which can still work. The obvious example in most people's lives is falling in love. There is no rulebook for this, no blueprint, no guarantees. Often there is no reason to it at all. But when we have fallen for someone, we know it. And it is an unstoppable feeling that overrides all of our instincts of caution and self-preservation. There is jeopardy in love because we might be rejected and it could all go pear shaped in the end, but it can also be one of the most exhilarating things in your life. And you can't have that if you aren't prepared to both give up some of your inhibitions to take the risk of having your feelings hurt, and to give passion a chance.

Ignoring evidence

The Black Farmer may be a name that is fundamentally about my story and my passions in life, but the idea for it actually came from my neighbours in Cornwall, when

I bought my farm in the late 1990s. They hadn't seen a black farmer before, so that is what they started to call me. And as far as I was concerned, it seemed like a bloody good brand name. Just like Richard Branson in the 1960s, when the word virgin was not something people were comfortable saying out loud, it had a risqué element that I thought would get through to people. At worst, they would stop and think about it a little: should they really be saying those words? Wasn't it offensive? At best, they would be intrigued, and want to find out the story behind the name.

I was convinced, but when we put the name out for market testing, the recommendation came back that we should avoid it. The name was too risky, I was told; some people were offended by it and we couldn't afford to risk putting off potential customers at point of sale. On instinct, I knew the advice was wrong. There might well be some logical hurdles and objections to The Black Farmer as a name, but I had already convinced myself that its fundamental power could overcome them. It was so distinctive, so true to the business I wanted to build, that I couldn't miss the chance of going with it. There was no better way of expressing my passion and personality, and embedding it in the business from day one.

So, I ignored that advice and the rest is history. Had I gone for something more politically correct – called it the Afro-Caribbean Farmer, for example – we would never have had the same traction in the market. And had I followed the advice of the market researchers, we would have ended up with something that might have pleased a focus group dedicated to the task, but never have got anywhere with capricious consumers whose attention has to be hard earned before they even start to think about you. I knew The Black Farmer was our best chance, because it was a name with jeopardy: one that challenged convention and made a bold play for market attention. And it was something that allowed me to express the passions that I wanted to pour into building this company.

Ignoring the market research was the best decision I have ever taken in business. It also, for me, symbolises one of the great battles that anyone seeking to live a life with jeopardy must understand: logic versus passion. Today we are living in a society, especially in the UK, where logic and reason are becoming the dominant factors in how we think and make decisions, while instinct and passion take a back seat. In business, especially, it is becoming all about the data, how much information you can amass and feed into the machine, to tell you what you should be thinking and doing.

On the face of it, there is nothing wrong with that. Of course we want evidence as a basis for how businesses act, governments form policy and individuals make life choices. Yet it is the fallacy of an advanced society to believe that we can outsource our decisions to research, data and technology. The global financial system collapsed a decade ago because too many bankers had become used to trusting what their algorithms were telling them, and suspended their judgement as a result. Politicians, from Hillary Clinton in the USA to Theresa May in the UK, have come a cropper because their carefully focus-grouped slogans have been made to look robotic in the face of more passionate opponents.

These are uncertain times for those in politics, business and beyond who always assert that they have fact and reason on their side. We are seeing more and more the limits to an outlook on life that is focused-grouped, scientifically tested and endlessly predicted. That doesn't mean we should ignore data, but nor should we pretend that it isn't often wrong, or used to draw the wrong conclusions. As we have seen with political polling, when the numbers don't add up to the consensus view, sometimes the professionals producing them will manipulate those figures – coming up with ever more elaborate mechanisms to explain their work – until they match expectations.

Sometimes the strength of an idea, a belief and a passion can override a consensus, however deeply rooted that is. That has been the clarion call of outsiders and innovators throughout history. And for those wanting to achieve big dreams, it is something that must be a fundamental belief. Those who would rely a hundred per cent on the data are seeking to strip away jeopardy, but those who want to do what the mainstream cannot must live with risk. They must find and harness the power of passion.

Being unprofessional

Part of the jeopardy of being a person with passion is that it doesn't fit easily with the norms and expectations of our working culture. We are used to this idea of being 'professional', buttoned up and deferential in the business environment. Of not being the person we really are, but a version of ourselves that will fit in with our idea of what it is to be 'at work'. By contrast, people who show emotions are often looked down on: the phrase 'you're being emotional' is one that will only ever be used negatively, discrediting passion rather than encouraging it. That arises from a prevailing wisdom in business that facts should come before feelings. People want evidence, not emotion, and are often embarrassed or confused when they have to deal with the alternative. Think about how we use the word 'dispassionate' to signify objectivity and independence, and the implications then of displaying actual passion.

This is particularly prevalent in UK society, where social norms and office politics restrain how we do our jobs: often we will bite our lips rather than say the idea that is on our minds, or we will undercut ourselves through self-deprecation. Anything to avoid the jeopardy of putting your ideas and opinions out in the open where they, and you, can be attacked from all sides by people who only ever speak out from the safety of the consensus view, attacking the new idea of someone who has dared to stray beyond it.

My advice is to forget about that. Does it really matter if people disagree with you or laugh in your face? Doesn't it say a lot more about them than you? If people only put their ideas out there when they were sure of the response, many of our greatest inventions would never have been created, and the world would be a much poorer place.

The fact is, if you want to move forward in your life, you need to get past the embarrassment threshold of giving voice to your ideas and passions, however silly or outlandish they may seem. When I was working in catering, doing a job that was never going to fulfil me, the thing I fell in love with in my spare time was watching documentaries on television. That, I thought to myself, would be something I would love to do.

On the face of it, this was another of my mad ideas. Remember that I had no qualifications, no experience, no connections. And the BBC, which was the only obvious place to go then, was not a place where people like me worked, at least not in the jobs that I aspired to. I could have easily had a menial, support staff role, but the idea of being a producer or a programme editor was pretty out-landish. It was public school and Oxbridge all the way, and I had hardly been to school, let alone one that I could trade off. (In fact, much later, when I was working there, some-one did ask me what school I had been to. The question wrong-footed me – I genuinely didn't know what they were getting at – and my answer, Oldknow Secondary Modern, drew an equally confused response.) I was the worst candi-date in the world for the BBC's graduate scheme as it then stood. I shouldn't even have been thinking about trying, but I had a consuming passion to make this happen, to escape the catering world and to do something that I knew I would love. I put aside the doubts in my mind, pretended to ignore the very obvious and steep hurdles that stood in my way and set about getting myself the job I dreamed of.

A dream is not a fairytale, however, and winning that job didn't happen overnight: I wrote to every producer and director whose details I could find in the *Radio Times*, and I phoned everyone whose number I could get hold of. There was not a single response to any of the letters, and no one who mattered would agree to take my calls. Then I befriended everyone I could find who had any connection with the BBC at all: cleaners, security guards, you name it, I tracked them down. And I finally got my break. Someone took pity on me, and I finally won an introduction to a great man named Jock Gallagher, later the head of BBC Radio. He was the one who took a chance on me, one of the guardian angels who made a real difference in my life and opened doors that I never could have opened on my own.

It wasn't just brute force determination and persistence that got me that opening. It's all very well to say that if you try hard enough, you will always succeed, but that just isn't true. What made the difference was that I had real passion. I was selling the only asset I had, and that was my story: something authentic, different and completely true. Something that no CV, however impressive and polished, could convey. That was what earned me my chance and, really, laid the foundations for the all good things that were to follow. It was my obvious, desperate passion that led Jock to give me a shot, even when I had none of the on-paper requirements. It would have been very easy for me to have given up. There were plenty of moments when I was getting nowhere and it felt like a fool's errand. But I kept going, and I finally found someone who believed in me and was willing to give me that chance.

We will all need guardian angels like that to succeed in our lives. But unless you show that you have passion, really care about what you do and will do anything to succeed, then it is much harder for those people to find you, let alone believe in and put their trust in you. It is passion that must be your differentiator: the thing that makes you stand out, your one defence against irrelevance and obscurity. When nothing else is in your favour, and nobody is giving you a second thought, it is only passion that can make the difference. It is your most important asset when dealing with the challenges that a life with jeopardy throws at you.

The passion pact

You may be reading this thinking that you already have things you are passionate about in life. But I bet they have little or nothing to do with your work. If you go around your office and ask people what they are passionate about, most of the answers will be about leisure pursuits: sport, music, fashion, food and drink, film, literature. We give ourselves permission to be passionate about the things that we do for fun, but not those we do for a living.

Many of us would be embarrassed to say that we are passionate about what we do to pay the bills. We don't want our colleagues or friends to think of us as too keen, or that we live only for work. So we relegate passions into the realm of hobbies, things that have a place in our personal life, but which we leave at the door before coming into work.

If that is your view, you are severely limiting the chances of finding a job and career that fulfils you. It puts you firmly in survival mode, seeing your working life as something that is a simple means to an end, rather than an opportunity to pursue. That may, on the face of it, feel like the safe choice to make, one that helps you look after yourself and your family. But think of how much time you spend working, how much of your life you give to turning up and doing your job. Think of what you could achieve if you used that time to do something that made you feel alive.

To deny yourself passion in your professional life – which, by time expended, is the biggest part of your entire life – is pretty absurd when you stop to think about it. And yet many people still consider their jobs an inconvenience to get out of the way so they can enjoy the time they have left over with friends and family. They set out in their twenties to climb a particular career ladder and, by the time they realise they might not want it, they've gone so far that they get stuck. It's no wonder that, after a few decades on the hamster wheel, so many people finally get sick of it in their forties and fifties when the realisation that they have only so much time left kicks in.

It doesn't have to be that way, and you don't need to become one of those middle-aged commuters who goes to work every morning looking like they hate not just their job, but life itself. There is another choice, and that is to escape survival mode and to embrace passion. That will mean different things for different people. You might have always wanted to work in a different field, to start a business of your own, or to make a living from something that you have enjoyed doing for fun: music, cooking or painting for instance. The dream you have always harboured somewhere but been too scared to actually reach for.

Leaving behind the security of a job and salary to pursue your dream may seem like a huge risk, and it's true that it will often entail lots of difficult decisions. But unless you accept that jeopardy, you will never give yourself the chance to live the life you actually want. The decision you have to make is whether to let blunt logic be the determining factor, or whether to create some space to let your passions run wild, and to follow where they lead. A lot of people deny that doing this is even a possibility. They point to financial obligations, retraining difficulties and any number of factors that make it 'impossible' to fundamentally change their career. Yet, while this may be quite convincing up to a point, it is a trap of the individual's own making. Nothing is ultimately stopping you from making the change that will allow you to pursue a working life rooted in passion. There are factors that make it difficult, of course; that is the jeopardy you will face. But the only person really stopping you, ever, is yourself.

That doesn't necessarily mean that you can up sticks and make a change tomorrow. As I've said about my own experience, it can take years or even decades to fulfil a dream. You might need to invest time in earning more money, even if it's doing a job you don't enjoy. But when you are doing that for a reason, with a clear purpose in mind, it's a world away from when you were slogging away without an end in sight. It means, however boring or unfulfilling the work might be, that you are someone who has rekindled the fire of passion within yourself. You have motivation again, a reason to get up in the morning.

It's what I like to call the passion pact – the opposite of a survivor's pact that signs away the possibility of living your most interesting life in return for security and safety. The passion pact is a promise to focus all your energies on the things you most want to do and achieve in life; to give full expression to your dream, throwing yourself into doing something you think you will love. It's a pact that accepts the considerable jeopardy that comes with unleashing passion in your working life – renouncing the safety of the pack and perhaps the security of the salary – to pursue something that is really meaningful to you. It's a decision that will set you apart from old colleagues, and sometimes even friends and family, who may worry more about what you might lose than they appreciate what you can gain.

A passion pact is an agreement with, and commitment to, yourself to live the best life you possibly can, because you never know what might be around the corner. You never know how much time you, and the people you care about, actually have left to do the things that really matter. So if you want to make a change, if you want to break the cycle, then you have to grasp the nettle and unleash your passions in life. By doing so, you are taking another step towards the full embrace of jeopardy that is necessary to succeed.

CHAPTER 6

Enjoy uncertainty

If there is one thing that jeopardy guarantees, and which you will encounter in spades by following your dreams and your passions, it is uncertainty. With jeopardy as your companion, you are frequently going to feel uncomfortable and unsure about yourself and the circumstances you find yourself in. There is going to be self-doubt and soul searching. Instability will become your new normal, but before you go running for the hills, let me take some time to explain why that is actually a very good thing.

I have lived with uncertainty my entire life. When you grow up poor, you never really know what is around the corner, what calamity may be about to strike, whether you're going to be able to pay that month's rent, or what you might have to go without next.

It won't surprise you to learn that a large part of my motivation in life has been about escaping that trap, about getting myself to a position where I can provide certainty for myself and my family, enough money to know that we're OK and can do the things we want. When you know what it is like to go without, you never want to find yourself in that position again, and you will do anything to prevent your children from having to experience what you did.

But as someone who has lived, at different times, with both real stability and instability in my life, I believe that you can have too much of a good thing. The security that comes with certainty can too easily become stagnation; the comfort it gives you can become a comfort zone that you struggle to escape. Someone whose life is entirely rooted in certainty – certainty of income, certainty of employment, certainty of financial security – is not a person who is likely to make great leaps or achieve innovative things. Why would they, when they already have so much of what a person could want in life? Why would you bother to take the risks of breaking a model that works for you?

No, if you want to really succeed in life and make the most of your talents, you need a little bit, and probably a lot, of uncertainty. You need financial uncertainty that motivates you to do more to make your own money; personal uncertainty where you push yourself beyond the limits of what you think you are capable of; and career uncertainty, where you do things that may harm your apparent short-term interest because they contribute to a greater dream.

Uncertainty is a part and parcel of pursuing your dreams and unleashing your passions in life. It is a core component of the jeopardy that you must embrace to get what you most want – the spur to push yourself into new, exciting and dangerous territory. For me, the jeopardy of uncertainty has proved one of the most important motivators and catalysts in my life. Escaping the uncertainty that I was born into, and constantly putting myself into new states of uncertainty – joining the BBC, starting my own business, buying the farm – because I knew they could lead me out of environments I wanted to escape and into places where I wanted to be.

With uncertainty, you give yourself that mental edge; the just-right dose of fear that allows you to get the best out of yourself. It doesn't matter how old or experienced you are, a dose of uncertainty can do wonders for you. This is how Steven Spielberg, the legendary film director, describes it: 'Every time I start a new scene, I'm nervous. And when that verges on panic, I get great ideas.' Even someone as successful and seasoned as he is still gets huge benefit from the jolt of uncertainty that comes with venturing into the unknown.

This is the opposite of being stuck and complacent in a job you know you can do well. When you're uncertain about what you are doing, and your own ability to succeed, then you are in a place where you can really learn and improve. The most important strides you make in life are when you put yourself in situations where you aren't comfortable and don't have certainty, but manage to survive, learn and, in the end, prosper.

When you embrace uncertainty, whether that is in your personal life or your career, you are putting yourself in a situation where you have no option but to move forwards. You are closing the door behind you on a safe, stable and staid approach to life. You're stepping out into unchartered territory, and once you've taken that first step, then you are more likely to take the next. Through the necessity of making progress, you are creating the hunger to succeed, just as living in a comfort zone saps the will to experiment and innovate.

Of course, when I talk about embracing uncertainty, it suggests that there might be a choice in the matter, which is really no longer the case. We are not living in a world in which you can decide between living in your comfort zone and venturing out into the brave unknown. At a time where technology is changing faster than ever before, and with political uncertainty of all sorts prevalent, there is less basis than ever before for believing that you can keep hold of the life and career you have today, now and into the future. As we undergo what is likely to be the biggest automation of jobs since the Industrial Revolution, no part of the economy is going to be protected from massive change. No job will be sheltered from either being radically transformed or made redundant.

Jeopardy is going to play an ever-greater part in all our lives as the pace of change and the degree of uncertainty increases. The truth is that we are all going to face uncertainty, whether or not we stay doing the same things as before, or decide to make a change. So the question is really whether you are someone who will proactively take hold of uncertainty, make it your friend and turn it to your advantage, or someone who is going to sit back and let it happen to you. Uncertainty is going to find you one way or another, whether that is technological change affecting your work, or something totally unexpected happening in your life. It will be much better if, by the time it does, you are ready for it.

The unknown quantity

Everything I have ever achieved in life has come because I was prepared to throw myself into situations of uncertainty, in which I didn't know if I would be good enough to adapt and survive. Joining the army was quite a step for a boy from the wrong side of Birmingham – one who didn't like authority or being told what to do. Starting at the BBC, even once I'd worked so hard to get my foot in the door, was daunting in its own different way. There, in amongst people with all the elite training and social skills in the world, I was the roughest of rough diamonds, with no qualifications, crippling dyslexia and zero experience in the world of television. It was the same when I came to start my first business: I'd never run anything myself (except a production shoot) and I had no experience of marketing. It was no different when I founded The Black Farmer: the logistics of running a fresh produce brand were entirely new to me, even if by now I had plenty of experience on the promotional side.

Anyone who has ever achieved anything in business, science, sport or politics has at some point felt this way: completely unsure as to what they were meant to be doing, and if they would be any good at it. But what sets apart those who succeed, by and large, is that they don't let that uncertainty stop them from keeping on going. Uncertainty helps determine what kind of person you want to be:

are you someone who shrinks away from it, or who gets excited by the possibility of doing something new? Does that slightly sick feeling in the pit of your stomach, the one we all get when we are at the limits of our comfort zone, motivate you or make you afraid? It may be a mixture of the two, and there is nothing wrong with that. There is certainly nothing wrong with being afraid, as long as it is not the fear that paralyses you and prevents you from taking action, because when you are faced with uncertainty there are only two possible reactions: run towards it, or run away from it. If you want to do the former, then you will need two things: a willingness to fail, and an appetite to learn.

You need a willingness to fail, because there is no serious endeavour in life in which success can be guaranteed. Anyone who tells you otherwise is a liar. When you are trying to do something new, like launching a business into a competitive market, or building a career where many others are vying to take your place, there is a good chance that you will fail. Of course, failure can be relative; it probably won't mean your ending up destitute, but it could be that you won't succeed to the degree that you had hoped. In any case, you have to be ready for it – both for the disappointment you will feel, and to pick yourself up off the floor and plan your next move: how you are going to get back on the horse and keep going.

One of the great things about failure is that it is a teacher. You learn more from the things you get wrong, from the times you don't get the job, lose the new business pitch or get outgunned by a competitor who thought of an idea first or executed it better. You learn because failure makes you look at yourself, scrutinise what you did and didn't do, and then resolve to do things differently the next time. Failure provides the motivation to get better, and if you are working too hard to mitigate the possibility that it will ever happen, then you are also depriving yourself of one of the most important learning opportunities there is.

With success, there is a level of complacency that starts to creep into your mindset, however hard you try to stop it. Why get better when what you do is good enough already? If you are operating at a level that means you succeed almost every time, then you have entered the seductive, but ultimately dangerous, land of certainty. Your appetite is sated and your capacity for improvement blunted. By contrast, while the uncertainty of new challenges may seem more treacherous, it is actually the safer option if your aim is to progress in your life and career. People who are constantly putting themselves into situations where they feel a little uncomfortable, a little underqualified, are those who change how they operate, keep getting better and ultimately have the last laugh. They might have a tougher time of it, but they will – with perseverance – be rewarded for embracing uncertainty and treating it as the friend and teacher that it can be. For though we have some things to fear in uncertainty, and that is entirely natural, we have far, far more to learn from it. And those who make that realisation – really take it to heart and start living by it – have taken one of the most meaningful steps towards achieving their dream.

False certainty

In the end, your ability to cope with uncertainty has a lot to do with the attitude you show towards it. A good test would be to fill a room half with entrepreneurs and half with senior managers from corporations. If you gave them all a briefing on an exciting new product or market for expansion, I can almost guarantee that the response would be evenly split. The entrepreneurs would talk about opportunity, the chance to get out ahead of the competition, seize the moment and rapidly build market share. The corporates would probably acknowledge the opportunity too. But the next word out of their mouths would be about risk: mitigation and management. Their starting point would be about what there is to lose, where entrepreneurs – the true champions of uncertainty in business – would focus almost entirely on what there is to gain.

Let me illustrate with a few examples from my own company. All Black Farmer sausages are gluten free. Today that is an entirely unexceptional statement. Most of our competitors can say the same. The market for gluten-free produce has exploded over recent years; indeed, in 2016 it was the fastest growing of all packaged food categories right across the world. You can see it with your own eyes in any supermarket: row upon row of gluten-free products, where a decade ago you would have been lucky to find any, and even then they would have been tucked away in the furthest corner.

This now rapidly expanding market was once just a speck on the horizon of the food and drink industry.

When we did the original market research back in 2004, it showed that around one in a hundred people had some kind of wheat intolerance, but suggested that, as a lifestyle choice, it was something that was starting to become more mainstream. We might have thought nothing of it – it was far from a hot issue or major growth area at the time, and the business case for it was a long way from being the overwhelming argument that it has since become. At that point it was the idea of organic produce that dominated most of the market's thinking; Duchy Originals was the premium brand of choice, and we were being told that marketing the product as organic was the only way to go. Organic offered certainty; we knew that people were already buying into it. But the parallel problem with that was that the niche had been filled, and the competition was already in place and well established. It would be much harder to build a quick following there than in virgin territory, which is what gluten free then represented. So I saw an opportunity: both to take advantage of a market segment that appeared to be on the verge of real growth, and also to offer something to people who were currently being poorly served by the existing market. Why should those with coeliac disease have to eat a special, separate product from the rest of their family, when it was perfectly within our power to create sausages that were top quality and also happened to be gluten free? We compromised nothing on taste but opened up a whole new area of the addressable market.

Today an estimated eight and a half million people in the UK, well over ten per cent of the overall population, live a gluten-free lifestyle. And, of course, now every major brand in our space caters for them, because it would be foolish not to. After the brand name, the decision to go gluten free was one of the most important we took in the early days, because it gave us something distinctive beyond being just another sausage brand. It was a decision based partly on research, but also a large dose of instinct. It felt like the right call and I liked that it put us on the side of people who were not being well served. There was uncertainty in it, of course, but what I really saw was the opportunity to differentiate ourselves from the get-go, to make a positive statement about who we were and whose side we were on.

Now, if I had been one of the really established players in our market, like Walls or Richmond, it would have been a very different decision. There's no way you could have made your products gluten free at the drop of a hat. It would have been a decision carefully weighed up, and probably done via launching a separate product rather than messing with the original version. The uncertainty of what existing customers would think, and the difficulty of changing the production process, would have prevented them from making such a bold move. If it ain't broke, don't fix it.

It is a classic example of seeing false certainty in the present, while talking down the opportunities of tomorrow and overplaying the risks involved. The most seductive fallacy in business is to believe that things will, generally speaking, continue the way they are, and that change is riskier than plotting a steady, unchanging course. Yet, as the sausage market itself has demonstrated over the last decade, by far the greatest risk is to sit on your hands and hope that change will never come. In 2015, UK consumers bought an estimated two billion fewer sausages than they had in 2008. The very same health reasons that are driving people towards the gluten-free lifestyle were moderating appetites for the traditional banger – all of which means that brands have to adapt, and fast, to changing tastes. It's not enough to follow in behind these trends. The consumer does not wait for you, and nor will the competition. You have to make your move while there is still uncertainty over where exactly the pieces will fall. And that means there isn't always an entirely watertight, de-risked business case to be made at the point where you really have to make your decision. The gluten-free gambit paid off because we were ahead of the trend, not so far ahead that the customers weren't there, but enough to allow us to be first, with all the advantages that brings.

We haven't always got it right, however: we suffered from one classic moment of indecision ourselves, a few years ago. This was the time when the chicken sausage was about to enter the mainstream, with health-conscious consumers looking to marry their love of sausages with a lower-fat alternative. Again, this was an opportunity that we had in our sights and one I was keen to pursue. But I ran into a problem because our manufacturers simply didn't agree. They took a much less instinctive, more numbers-based approach: it's a tiny part of the market, they said. Let's focus on the big stuff that matters. If competitors want to have a go, then let them.

The problem with that sort of approach is that it is based on the idea that fundamental change is not going to happen. It assumes that market segments that are small will always remain small. And it wants to set aside the uncertainty of a new opportunity for the familiarity of known territory. In the end, their view held sway and we didn't launch a chicken product at that point. One of our main competitors, as we knew they were planning, did so and had great success with it. And, although we have since produced our own, the opportunity to be first to market had gone, because the case for certainty had overcome the argument for embracing uncertainty and trying something new.

My experiences in both seizing and missing opportunities with The Black Farmer have brought home to me how important it is to have a mindset that views uncertainty as not just positive, but entirely necessary. Today's business landscape is one in which change is so rapid and so constant that, unless you are changing too, you are almost certainly failing to respond to new trends and market demand. Unless you show the willingness to embrace uncertainty by trying new things, backing your instincts and intuition even when not all the numbers may add up, you will be falling behind. Uncertainty may seem like the risky option, but the real dangers are in pretending that the certainties of yesterday will still hold good now and into the future. And that is every bit as true for an individual plotting their career path as a business looking towards its future sales targets.

The only certainty

There is nothing new about people and companies struggling in the face of change, either denying its existence, or ridiculing innovations that have proved to be defining. From the automobile to the iPhone, some of the most important inventions have been written off in their early days by the so-called experts, who thought they could never displace the horse and cart or the dumbphone. Sometimes, even when the future is right under someone's nose, they will turn away from it. Perhaps the most famous example of this in business is Kodak, which invented digital photography in the 1970s but put the technology in a drawer because they were afraid of cannibalising their core camera-film business. It quite literally created the tool for its own destruction, then hid from it, rather than embracing the new possibilities that it created. Bankruptcy ultimately followed for what had been one of the world's most iconic brands and greatest innovators.

If you try and deny the future, and create a permanent certainty of the present, then you are doing the commercial equivalent of seeking to defy gravity. You might stay airborne for a time, but in the end the only way is down. The status quo, if it ever really existed in business, is less lasting and more volatile than ever before. It is not something that can be relied upon, but which must be constantly reinvented. A company that chases change can fail every bit as much as one that seeks to cling to the present; the only difference is that it has given itself a chance of success, a foothold in the future, however precarious.

Companies that are not prepared to embrace such uncertainty are almost certainly consigning themselves to the dustheap, even if it may prove to be a slow death.

All of this means that uncertainty is the only certainty in today's business landscape, and the winners will be those who learn to navigate it. The real risk lies in trying to keep hold of what you have and to preserve your gains, rather than grabbing hold of the uncertainty that is inevitable. No business or business model is safe in a world where the pace and scale of change is so significant. Even a company like Uber, one of the world's fastest-growing, is already investing heavily into a future – of driverless cars – that is entirely at odds with its current structure.

There is huge success to be had, and fortunes to be made, for people who have the vision and imagination to see how fundamentally different our world will be in a relatively short space of time. You only have to watch *Back to the Future* or read articles from the early days of the Internet to see how bad we are at predicting the changing nature of the way we live and do business. You will find a mixture of things that have already become obsolete by their supposed arrival date, and others that are probably never going to happen. When the iPhone arrived just over a decade ago, people got very excited about what was largely seen as a new generation of mobile phone, which allowed Internet and emails on the go. Few fully foresaw the total revolution that smartphones would create and how, within a few years, we would be running so many aspects of our lives out of our back pocket.

Just as uncertainty has undermined some established

business models, it has also created a huge market for new ones aimed squarely at the consumers of our mobile age. From taxi apps to delivery services, mobile banks and online retailers, this is a boom time. Change has rewarded those who have seen excitement and opportunity in uncertainty, and built new models to take advantage, rather than trying to shore up those whose natural environment is fast receding. And, in turn, everything – from the way we shop and watch television, to how we stay in touch with our friends and family – has changed.

In truth, we are only at the beginning of the revolution in how technology can change the way we live. It's a tide that spells trouble for the big establishment players across a whole range of fields, those whose hold on their markets had until recently seemed unshakeable. From banks to supermarkets and utilities, gatekeepers that have acted as the sole intermediary for their customers are now being threatened by any number of more nimble, agile competitors that offer people a more direct relationship with what they are buying and who they buy from.

If you take supermarkets, for instance, there has already been a huge shift as relatively recent entrants such as Aldi and Lidl have eaten into the market share that the likes of Tesco had come to take for granted. The established players thought they had created an impregnable fortress: one based around stripping away brands, investing heavily in own-label products and amassing huge amounts of customer data through loyalty schemes such as Clubcard. All that, wrapped together with the promise of being the best value. Yet when the discounters came along and undercut them on price, they were left scrabbling to find a differentiator. The world they had created, and which they thought was never going to change, was suddenly looking very uncertain.

This is just the beginning. We are only in the foothills of change in the food retail sector. The move of major technology players like Amazon into the space shows what the future might start to look like. In the end, supermarkets gained their supremacy by being the ultimate convenience, bringing together everything under one roof, at a great price. Yet if that convenience can be outstripped by on-demand delivery, then there will be no need for supermarkets anymore, all of which spells trouble for those sitting on top of a legacy model with huge property portfolios. It also creates huge possibility for producers who may be empowered to find a new, more direct relationship with their customers.

As Einstein didn't quite say, for every moment of uncertainty there is an equal and opposite window of opportunity. Those who embrace the uncertainty and jeopardy of the moment will overcome competitors who try and manage it out of their businesses and lives. The only question is, which side are you going to be on, and how can you react to take advantage?

Comfortable discomfort

The big picture of coming uncertainty is important, because, distant at it may seem, it is something that affects us all, whether we are business owners or career professionals, whether just starting out in working life or several decades in. The necessity of embracing uncertainty, of letting jeopardy into our lives, is universal. What, then, can you start to do to embrace uncertainty in your life, your career and, if you have one, your business? If change is a given, how do you turn it to your advantage? My advice is to try and find a sweet spot between the things that make you a bit queasy with uncertainty and those that simply terrify you; and between what the data and research is telling you to do, and the opportunities that your gut is urging you to pursue.

In the end, your appetite for change is going to come down to what you have to lose, and how much you fear losing it. One of my great advantages in life is that I came from nothing, so I know what it is like to be in a situation where you have lost everything (or rather in my case, to have never had it). That does inoculate you to some extent against the fear of total destitution; because if you have climbed the ladder once, you know that you can look after yourself. When you have known what it is like to be at the bottom of the pile, you fear it less than those who never have.

By the same token, if the thought of losing the safety and security you already have terrifies you, then you are probably not going to get very far, because fear will be inhibiting you more than it motivates you. Everyone's circumstances are different, and it would be foolish of me to pretend that everyone should throw all the pieces of their life and career in the air, and hope they land the right way. Instead, you have to make a judgement based on your own circumstances and mindset, getting to a level of discomfort you can live with, and which will motivate you to keep pushing on, learning and improving. You have to embrace a level of uncertainty that allows you to bring out the best in yourself, a level at which you think it's going to be hard, but that there is always, somehow, somewhere, a way through.

The trick is to find a level of challenge that puts you on the edge, but doesn't push you over it. That might mean applying for a new position at the place where you work, rather than leaving entirely. Or making a plan for what you are going to change before you rush into it. If you are looking to start a business, it might mean finding a partner who makes up for some of the knowledge and expertise you may lack.

But remember this: most of us overestimate the dangers of making a big change and underestimate our ability to make it work. Just as you wouldn't bid your maximum first time when buying a house, you almost certainly won't be ambitious enough when thinking about how to embrace change and uncertainty in your life. You may think first about what there is to lose, and what is likely to go wrong. There's nothing wrong with that, but you have to learn to push those feelings to one side and create space to dream about what could go right: the opportunities there to be pursued, and the excitement to be had in chasing your dream. Make sure you push yourself a bit further than you were initially prepared to go. Allow yourself to imagine the full scope of what you could achieve before you start imposing restrictions and limitations on yourself. Travel the journey in your mind; think what it would look and feel like. Imagine what others would say. Focus for a moment just on the upside. And then, only then, should you start to be 'realistic', to stress test your ideas and examine the obstacles in your way. That is an important part of the process, but if it is your starting point, then you are never going to get as far as you could. Big dreams do not begin from a place of logic and reason, though they ultimately need to be anchored in them. The important thing is to not allow rationality and caution to clip your wings before you have even begun to take flight.

The other crucial necessity for thriving in a world of uncertainty is that you believe in yourself. It is very easy to focus only on the things you cannot do (or which you think you can't do) and to ignore the skills and experience you actually have. At the same time, many of us give too much credit to friends and colleagues who seem confident and unbeatable, but who, of course, have just as many flaws and problems as you do. We are all a mixed bag of talents and attitudes, some useful and others unhelpful. No one is the perfect mix, which is why you ultimately need to build a team of others around you to complement your strengths and make up for your weaknesses. But when it is just you, the thing that matters is focusing on what you can do well. It is a hard enough road when you believe in yourself completely, and if you do not, then you are giving yourself next to no chance.

Above all, when thinking about uncertainty, remember this. You are not alone in being afraid of change and worried about what it means for your business or career.

There are a lot of people thinking about the same problems and opportunities, but who will sit on their hands, doing nothing about it, because, in the end, a lot of people – and the same goes for companies – are waiting for someone else to take the lead, to test the waters and prove the concept. They want others to make the unchartered territory safe before they venture into it. And they are the people who will struggle to achieve their goals, and the businesses who will tend to fall by the wayside. While it might feel like the safe option, you don't get credit for being late to the party. You just end up at the back of a very long queue. So, if you are someone who wants to propel themselves and their business to the front, you need to be the pioneer who embraces uncertainty, not the latecomer who only shows up when it's safe to do so. In business, and in life in general, people follow a leader. And you need to decide whether you want to be the one doing the leading or the following. Uncertainty is the litmus test that helps you to decide.

CHAPTER 7

Get an attitude problem

If you are an entrepreneurial person (and that can be anyone), then you will be used to one very frequent experience. It goes a bit like this: 'I'm sorry, but the answer is no'. It is the sickly taste of rejection, one that will become all too familiar if you are trying to build a business, or to do something daring in the job you have. By asking unusual questions, making unlikely demands and trying uncertain things, you put yourself firmly in the realm of rejection. People might not understand what you are trying to do, they may not like your idea, they might feel threatened by it, or they might just not have the time or inclination to even consider it. The easiest response is to reject it outright.

Rejection is what I got in spades when I was working so hard to break into the world of television. It's something I got used to when I started my marketing company and was on the constant hunt for clients. And it became like a close relative when I was trying to get my Black Farmer sausages listed by the major supermarkets in the early days. Some rejections are more direct than others (I had my fair share of people telling me over the phone that their boss was out of the office, not realising that they had failed to put me on hold while they chatted to them), but they all feel the same.

Embracing jeopardy is not a path that lends itself to having lots of people agree with you and clap you on the back. Whatever dream you are pursuing, the natural consequence of trying something new and different is that people will say no to you and your idea.

So what do you do? How do you overcome this tidal wave of indifference when you are in the early stages of pursuing your dream? The answer lies in the piece of advice my father once gave to me, the thing he used to say when I was a child dreaming about escaping the poverty of inner-city Birmingham. Whatever your circumstances, he told me, whatever qualifications you have in life, you can achieve anything you want if you have two things. The first is absolute, ruthless focus on your goals, to the exclusion of everything that distracts you from achieving them. And the second is an equally relentless positive attitude, because if you have that, then things come your way.

It might sound simplistic, for there are many more aspects to success than this. A business or career is not powered by willpower alone, but this does not diminish the central importance of attitude in achieving your dreams. It is the key that unlocks the door behind which everything else lies, the prerequisite before anything else is going to matter. Without a positive attitude, there isn't much point turning up in the first place. Attitude matters so much because, if you have chosen the path of jeopardy, it is inevitable that you will encounter obstacles as a daily occurrence. The steeper the mountain you seek to climb, the greater the number of hurdles you will find placed in your way. It is not the presence of those barriers that will determine the outcome, but how you respond to them. The attitude you show in the face of improbability, rejection and adversity is what matters above all.

This is about more than the simple notion that perseverance will always deliver results. It is a more deep-seated mindset: the way you approach your work, how you respond when things go wrong, your manner in dealing with others. A positive attitude is not just about being mindlessly cheerful and plugging away. It is about an outlook on life and business that is fundamentally forward looking: you don't get mired in problems, but look for solutions instead; you don't let setbacks derail your progress; and you treat people as prospective allies rather than potential enemies. Your attitude determines how you approach every day of your working life. It is about how you get stuff done.

Take the business meeting, for instance – that much-maligned, often-hated part of many of our daily lives. It is quite possible to spend far too much of your working life stuck in conference rooms with people who are doing little more than passing the buck and playing for time. You, however, can treat that time – when you have the right people together in one place – as an opportunity to drive forward progress, come up with new ideas and generate energy, in yourself and the people around you. It is all about attitude. Go into that meeting with the presumption that it will be a waste of time and it will almost certainly pan out that way. Go into it with the determination that it will be useful and a very different result may occur. That power is in your hands, and it is the same with every decision and interaction you have over the course of every working day; you get out what you put in. Your attitude sends a signal to the rest of the world about whether you are someone who means business or just another clock-watcher waiting for the day to end.

The American psychologist Professor Michael Scheier, who helped pioneer scientific research into the power of optimism in the 1980s, has summarised very well why a positive attitude really matters. He says this: '[We] know why optimists do better than pessimists. The answer lies in the differences between the coping strategies they use. Optimists are not simply being Pollyannas; they're problem solvers who try to improve the situation. And if it can't be altered, they're also more likely than pessimists to accept that reality and move on ... Pessimists, on the other hand, tend to deny, avoid and distort the problems they confront, and dwell on their negative feelings.'

For me that sums it up. If you have chosen to live a life with jeopardy, you will need to become very good at coping with setbacks and unexpected difficulties. Progress is hard enough even when you have the positive attitude to help you come up with solutions and give you the energy to keep on going. With the wrong attitude, you are going to get stuck very quickly, deflated by the inevitable disap-pointments you will encounter and lacking the emotional energy needed to overcome those obstacles in your way. A positive attitude is your armour against criticism, rejection and failure. It is the voice that tells you the idea is still a good one, that there will be a market for it, and that you are the right person to deliver it.

The Australian cricketer Richie Benaud, later a famous commentator, once said about captaincy that its success is ten per cent down to skill, and ninety per cent due to luck. In my view, success in life and business is ninety per cent determined by attitude. You can have all the talent, experience and connections in the world. It won't count for anything if you don't have the attitude to succeed. You need a real inner steel and determination, allied with the positive outlook on both your successes and your failures, and a proactive approach to dealing with opportunities and challenges alike. When you are letting jeopardy into your life and taking the necessarily hard road towards achieving your dreams, you need every bit of help you can get. And the best way to help yourself is with the right attitude.

Finding motivation

Attitude is not something we are born with, but which develops through our experiences. Babies do not emerge from the womb as pessimists, and as young children we are, if anything, largely inclined towards optimism. The attitudes that define our lives are in large part imposed upon us: expectations that others have of us, the pigeon hole that society seeks to place us in. As a poor, black boy from Birmingham, I was expected not to exceed the boundaries of my race and place in society. My lot was to take one of the low-skilled jobs that people like me were meant to have, and to go no further. Throughout my life, I have worked to reject those boundaries and overcome the barriers that people, knowingly or not, have put in my way.

The attitude that has driven me since those days has been about being a pioneer and a pathfinder – for myself and people like me: other poor kids, other black men, other school rejects, other dyslexics. It was pioneering to get into the BBC with my limited education and qualifications; pioneering to produce and edit television as someone who really struggled just to write scripts; pioneering to take myself to a part of the country where there were (and still are) very few people like me, to buy the farm and build the brand that I have. I say that not to pat myself on the back, but to highlight the fundamental importance of attitude in achieving the things you want in life. If you want to, it is possible to achieve things that no one believes a person like you is capable of. (And those people may include you!) It is possible to break new ground and overcome barriers. It is possible to change norms – not easy, but possible, if you have the right attitude, keep going through adversity and get just enough help and good luck along the way.

Attitude isn't just about being upbeat in the face of adversity and looking on the bright side of disappointments. It is also about your overarching view of the world and approach to life; and it can come from all sorts of different places and be motivated by all sorts of different things. For me, the fundamental attitude that has driven every decision I have taken has been to stick up two fingers to the assumptions that people and society had about me. I wanted to prove that I could live the life I wanted, pursue my dreams, and defy the low expectations that surrounded me, my family and my friends growing up. I could have let those expectations define me, but inside they provided even more motivation, a profound hunger to prove wrong those bastards and bigots who thought I was a hopeless case who would never find his way out of the ghetto, let alone achieve anything meaningful.

I have talked already about dreams and passion, about looking inside yourself to work out what matters most to you and what you want to achieve in life. Attitude is their close and crucial cousin, the real, burning motivation that both explains those dreams and passions and helps you begin the work needed to achieve them. It could be about proving other people wrong, proving yourself right or shocking the world. But as you start to sketch out your dream, one of the most useful things you can do is work out why you really want to do it in the first place. To establish the itch you are trying to scratch or the point you are desperate to prove. That is your motivation, the source of your fundamental attitude to life, and the thing you will need to fall back on in the toughest times. It, along with your dream, is what nobody can take away from you, however bad things may get. It will keep you going in good times and bad.

The power of attitude is such that it can derail your dreams as much as it can help achieve them. As a young man, it won't surprise you to hear that I was often angry at my life and the situation I found myself in. I hated authority, which is why I had such a tough time with the army – in retrospect, a choice that was never going to be a good fit. If I had just stayed angry, then I would not have achieved anything, except to antagonise myself and other people. But over time I learned that I could harness my anger into something more positive: a raging desire to break the mould of my expected life and achieve the things I most wanted.

This is what has allowed me to break barriers and redefine people's expectations of what a person from my background should be able to achieve. While, as I have mentioned, many around me disdained my dream of becoming a farmer and breaking into a white man's world, my attitude was always the opposite; that being an outsider is a strength not a weakness, and that the lack of others like me is not a reason to stop, but in fact an even greater motivation to try, so that the precedent can be set and others may be encouraged to follow. All this springs from the same place: the desire to prove wrong the expectations of others about me, and to show through example what can be achieved.

I would urge you to look within yourself, firstly to judge whether your attitude is setting you up to succeed, but also to work out what it is that really motivates you. Where can you find the internal energy and power that any person needs to succeed? What events in your life provide the source that can feed your ambitions and nurture your dreams? In the end, every successful person is motivated by something, somewhere: whether that is an event in their past or an external force they are trying to overcome. That motivation powers an attitude, which is what allows that person to get things done, overcome challenges and succeed. Before you can hope to do the same, you need to discover what truly motivates you and find a way to harness it to your advantage.

Adopting an open mind

On the road to finding that motivation and developing a better attitude in life, one of the most important tools in your armoury will be the power of an open mind. This may not sound like much, until you pause to consider quite how close-minded most people are about so many things. The way to test this is to try out an unusual new idea on your friends or colleagues. It could be for a new business you want to launch, or for a change in career path you are considering. You might well find a few people who support and encourage you, but I can almost guarantee that the majority will either dismiss it outright, or purse their lips and prevaricate over it, nitpicking the details and wallowing in what could go wrong as a result.

Most people who have started their own businesses or made significant changes in their lives have experienced this. The circle of concerned friends and family who don't think it's a good idea, and tug at your sleeve urging you to reconsider. They are people who have your best interests at heart, but in the end pay more attention to their own fears about the future than they do to your optimism or vision for it.

I found this not just when first talking about my dream to own a farm, but decades later when I was finally ready to fulfil it. Though attitudes to race had changed significantly in that time, many still warned me that the countryside, where there were and still are very few people of colour, would not welcome a black man. I can recall conversations with friends when I was just about to move down. They thought I was out of my mind. 'Don't they lynch people like you down there?' was how one put it. And he didn't actually use the words 'people like you'.

Yet I did not go to Devon either expecting or looking to find racism lurking around every corner. I could have bought into the assumption, mainly shared by people who have hardly set foot in a field themselves, that rural areas are backward by definition. Certainly, the idea that racism is pervasive in the countryside comes easily to those whose lives are primarily metropolitan. In 2004, the year I was getting The Black Farmer off the ground, the head of what was then known as the Commission for Racial Equality, Trevor Phillips, talked about there being a 'passive apartheid' in rural Britain, which understandably sparked a huge debate on both sides. That was a fairly typical metropolitan view and probably still is.

Instead I kept an open mind. I wanted to see the true situation for myself, and to see if it was possible to show that the people making assumptions were wrong, and that there is a place for people like me in areas we have not traditionally inhabited. What I discovered is that, irony of ironies, there was a lot more open-mindedness in the allegedly backward corners of rural Britain than in the big cities where the criticism came from. That is not to deny that problems exist or that some people have suffered abuse and discrimination. But, speaking purely for myself, while my arrival certainly caused a stir, I have not really experienced racism to my face since moving to the south-west (unless you count the person who asked me if I had come down to start a marijuana farm!). Indeed, I have not been racially abused in any circumstances for many years now. Instead, I have found people welcoming, curious and in large part supportive.

Because I started this crazy journey towards becoming a rural landowner with an open mind, I have been able to overcome people's expectations of what could be achieved. Together with my neighbours, newfound friends and those who supported me, I have demonstrated that there is an opportunity to become part of the rural community, something many had never thought possible or even desirable. Since then I have made it my mission to encourage others to follow. For a few years I ran a Black Farmer scholarship scheme, partly funded by one of Prince Charles's charities, which gave a group of young black people from 'up country' an experience of rural life. I knew how important it was to show young people the reality that lies behind the many assumptions that exist about being black in the countryside. While many in my community believe that doors are closed to them in society, that is as much a facet of being closed-minded as anything else. Discrimination does still exist, but so do the opportunities to transcend it if your attitude and commitment are right. On the other hand, when you start off with your mind closed to possibility, you see the barriers you wish to see, whether or not they are actually there in front of you. The truth is that the modern generation's grandparents and great-grandparents, the first-generation immigrants, were pioneers with huge bravery, who took their families into unfamiliar and sometimes hostile environments in search of a better life. There is nothing to stop any young black man or woman today doing the same. Once again, it comes down to attitude and an open mind above all.

An attitude problem

'You've got a bit of an attitude problem, but we're going to give you a go as a runner.' They were the words I had been waiting almost two years to hear. Jock Gallagher, my guardian angel at the BBC, was sitting behind his desk and telling me that I was being given a precious chance, something I had been working away to achieve for month after month, toiling fruitlessly up until that moment. It was the lowest rung, but I was on the ladder and determined to climb. From that position, I would eventually get onto the BBC's graduate training scheme (even though I hadn't really passed school, let alone university) and find my niche in food programming.

With that one sentence, Jock was doing more than give me my break. He was also foreshadowing my experience over a number of years with the BBC. The attitude 'problem' he identified was something that kept cropping up after that initial interview. It followed me round from department to department, from programme to programme, and I wore it like a badge of honour. For me, the only attitude I brought to the job was that no one was going to rob me of my chance and send me back to where I'd come from. And because I only had one shot, I was most definitely going to do it my own way.

What others called an attitude problem was for me about being creative, individual and single-minded in my vision of what good TV looked like and how to produce it. I didn't mind having a stand-up row with colleagues or talent about how a programme should work. For me, that was almost a part of the creative process, but it often brought me into conflict with colleagues who didn't appreciate my uncompromising approach. Unsurprisingly, it ruffled plenty of feathers and caused problems for me. Like a lot of large organisations, the BBC I knew wasn't somewhere you could really rise on talent alone. It was about people and politics: who knew whom, and who wanted to do a favour for – or do the dirty on – someone else. It was a game I was hopelessly ill-equipped to play; I didn't have the nous, the connections or the interest to do so. To be honest, I didn't really care because I was only there for one thing, and that was to make programmes I could be proud of and that people would watch. So what if I pissed a few people off along the way?

You cannot always afford to alienate people, and you certainly should not seek to when there is the opportunity to find a more consensual way, but sometimes you cannot avoid doing so, and in those circumstances, you should not shy away from the fight. When you hear people throwing the attitude problem grenade back at you, you know that you have touched a nerve. The fact is that 'attitude' is a very loaded word in the English language. People love the idea of positive attitude in principle, but if you are a person with attitude, that real edge and motivation, then you are going to encounter people who try and use it against you. It's one thing if you are lazing around, turning up late, not getting down to your work – that *would* be an actual attitude problem – but beware of those who reach for the same term to try and counter your good arguments and neuter your new ideas. Learn to recognise the signs and defend your corner against those who would seek to drag you down to their level.

Whatever others might try to say, attitude will always be one of your most important assets in life. You need it to live with jeopardy, but you will also discover that having attitude brings a new jeopardy all of its own. Because there are people who don't like it, don't know how to cope with it and whose instinctive reaction is to try and crush it. In those circumstances, you have to be single-minded and not fear doing things your way, however much some others may complain. In the end, you have to decide whether you are doing something to make friends or get results. While it can be possible to do both, it isn't always, and we shouldn't pretend otherwise. It's a fine line: revelling in having an attitude problem is going to very quickly turn you into a lone ranger without enough friends and supporters. But you must hold onto the outlook on life that makes you distinctive, even if it causes difficulties with the people around you. That is part of the jeopardy you must get used to, for most really good things come from a place of steadfast vision that will rally supporters but also provoke equally strong opposition. If you are to make progress, that is a level of conflict you must be prepared for.

Weakness or strength?

I did have my supporters at the BBC, however, and was lucky to have a succession of people who took me under their wing, helping to shield me from some of the brickbats that might otherwise have come my way. Most notable, after Jock, was Peter Bazalgette, who later became famous for introducing *Big Brother* to our screens and, more recently, was Chair of the Arts Council. He was another unconventional figure, someone who had his own way of doing things and who helped create space for people like me, protecting me from my critics.

It was at the BBC, under his and others' guidance, that I really started to recognise the importance of my status as an outsider, something I discussed earlier. It was the first time I had really strayed beyond the role in society I had been born into. Suddenly there I was, in amongst the middle-classes and the private school kids, at best a rough diamond, at worst a mouthy git who needed to be told when to shut up. What I discovered was that my being an outsider was far more a strength than it was a weakness. It meant that I thought and went about things in a different way from the vast majority of my peers. I was more direct and better able to get done the things I wanted to do. I had a clear view on how things should work and, because I wasn't afraid of offending people, was pretty direct in letting others know it, and in fighting my corner when I had to. Not being part of the club made it harder to break in, but once I was through the doors, it gave me all sorts of opportunities to stand out in the work I did. I wasn't just an outsider in my own right, I also ended up working in a sector that was a bit of an outcast: food and drink. In those days, food programming was yet to become the big business it is today. We had had Keith Floyd showing what was possible with his documentaries, but *Masterchef* had not yet aired and we were light years away from *Bake Off.*

Inside the BBC, most people's view was that this was the runt of the litter. They wanted to be working on current affairs documentaries, programmes like *40 Minutes* that were about hard news and global politics. By contrast, food and drink was not really seen as serious television. But I loved it. It was the chance to go all around the world, working with some brilliant chefs and producing television that I wanted to watch. We introduced people to the screen who would later become big names in the culinary world, like Gordon Ramsay, James Martin, Brian Turner and Antony Worrall Thompson. Having come from a catering background myself, it was no surprise to me that we often ended up having some pretty heated rows (which as far as I was concerned, was all the better). In something that others wanted to run a mile from, I found a vocation that I loved and cherished.

That, for me, is a great lesson, because I believe it shows again that attitude above all determines your ability to succeed. Do you accept what other people think and tell you, or do you back your own instincts and form your own view? I could have taken the attitude that I was being banished to the coldest, darkest corner of the BBC, which was certainly what some others wanted me to feel; instead I found something meaningful in it. In the same way, I could have let my status as an outsider deter me from making progress. Again, it turned out there was an opportunity hidden inside something that initially appeared to be a stumbling block. The same was true of my dyslexia, an initial weakness that sowed the seeds of a much greater strength.

I have encountered a similar situation in the farming world, where, as well as finding much warm support, I have come across some others who are resentful of me – a person who is not a 'proper' farmer – for the success I have had in building a brand and a business out of a tiny farm, while many are struggling to make their much bigger holdings profitable. My attitude in this world has always been that agriculture is a sector ripe for change, and that there is no use in people continuing to do as their parents and grandparents did before them, while the world changes around them and makes that livelihood more and more precarious. So many in that world are trapped by their old ideals, of a family business that is more about tradition than change. I believe that rural England needs to be much more radical in embracing change, from the way it markets itself to the people it encourages to make their lives here. For example, institutional landowners from local government to the Church could make much more of an effort than they currently do to encourage more diverse tenants who would represent the population at large, and who could bring new ideas and impetus. At the moment, they are more of a blockage than an enabler.

We are all dealt cards in life, in different ways at different times, but it is what we make of them that defines our ability to succeed. Our attitude – towards ourselves and other people, the circumstances and opportunities that surround us – is what determines the course of our lives. And that is something you must believe, otherwise you have no faith in your ability to set your own path in life. If that path is one with jeopardy, then you are going to need that fundamentally positive attitude even more.

So before we move on, try this quick exercise. Make a list of the things that are holding you back in life, those factors inhibiting you from achieving your dream. Now be honest with yourself. Which of the things you have written down are real roadblocks, actual immovable forces? And which of those, on reflection, exist more in your head than in reality? How many could be solved with the right attitude? If you are doing it right, you will end with a shorter list than you started with. And you will be on the way to making progress towards your dream.

CHAPTER 8

Develop a risk appetite

Almost anything we do in our everyday lives could be seen as a risk. We leave the house not knowing who or what we might encounter on our journey to work. We cross the road into the path of vehicles that could behave unpredictably. We put on the kettle and make a cup of tea with boiling water that could scald or maim us. We cook meals in kitchens full of sharp objects and heat sources that present a whole assault course of potential injuries.

Life is really nothing more than one big risk when you start to think logically about it. We are surrounded by the threat of danger in almost everything we do. Yet as humans we make a strange distinction: those things that we are used to we become comfortable with, to the point of complacency. Which is why people do get run over crossing the road, and do cut themselves when using kitchen knives. Most of those people probably weren't worried that something bad was about to happen before it did.

Present us with something unfamiliar, however, and our whole outlook changes. Suddenly we are professional risk-assessors, pointing out the things that could go wrong, the inherent dangers and the things we need to do to protect ourselves from harm. Probably no one has ever boarded a plane without giving some thought to the possibility of what could go wrong, but the facts tell us that you are more likely to die falling out of bed than in a plane crash – and no one watches a safety video before going to sleep at night. My point is that we are all natural risk-takers, even those who would describe themselves as cautious. We have simply stopped considering the everyday things we do as risks. They are normalised for us, and so are the dangers. So, when we talk about risk, often what we really mean is the unknown, the dangers of things that are not familiar, and those that we have never tried to do before.

Getting past that inhibition, that in-built caution, is something we must all do to achieve our dreams. Jeopardy means taking risks that fall into the unknown category, and one of the most important reasons to live with jeopardy is that it pushes you onwards to do things you would not otherwise undertake in your everyday life and work. It's how we learn, discover new things and get better.

Often the idea of risk is presented as something that some people shy away from while others, life's daredevils, run towards it. Yet risks are not absolute; it is how we perceive them that matters most of all. Very few people are going to do something if they believe it is likely to be harmful to them and their family. That isn't risk aversion, just common sense. Equally, something that is viewed as an opportunity first and foremost is not going to put many people off, even if it does contain some levels of danger and jeopardy.

To return to my previous theme, it is your attitude to risk that matters most above all. You need to know your limits, but you also need a clear-sighted, fundamentally positive approach to doing new and different things in your life. If all you ever see is risk and danger, then it will be hard to persuade yourself to give something a go.

Sharpening your risk appetite is really nothing more than getting used to a life where jeopardy is part and parcel of your everyday experience. One where you are constantly pushing yourself to do new things and experience novel environments. When you get yourself into that mentality, you normalise the process of taking risks and doing unusual things. Just as you boil the kettle or cross the road, you make big calls without missing a beat, because they are necessary for the growth of your business and the survival of your dream, just as leaving the house is to get to work in the morning.

As your circumstances and outlook change, and you progress further down the road to jeopardy, the relative balance of what appears risky changes too. When you are trying to build a new business, or get a challenging career off the ground, small steps will not carry you far. Indeed, they hold a greater guarantee of failure than the big leaps that are necessary for success against the odds. For what is really the greater risk: to fail while trying something daring, that at least carries the possibility of success, or to fall short because you hardly tried at all? Risk is always what we make of it, and sometimes the greatest danger lies in attempting to avoid it altogether.

Changing course

There is nothing I hate more in life than standing still. I believe there is actually no greater risk to an individual's sense of purpose, achievement and wellbeing than getting stuck in a job or life situation where you simply cannot make progress or achieve new things. It is this horrible feeling of wading through treacle, not being able to go anywhere or achieve anything of substance. Few people who have worked for any length of time will have totally avoided this. It is in the nature of modern life that we occasionally get overwhelmed and trapped by our circumstances. If you do, the important question is: what are you going to do about it?

When you are stuck you need an escape route, because it is in the jeopardy of the new – the search for different experiences, undiscovered limits and unmet people – that we really come alive. Then we are transformed, no longer zombies crawling through each day, but fully engaged with the people and opportunities around us. It is the chance to see the world in a totally different way, not through the jaded lens of the wage slave but through the fresh eyes of someone who is carving their own path in life.

After ten years with the BBC, I reached my own moment of dangerous calm. I had achieved much of what had initially driven me to pursue that career, making the documentaries I had once dreamed of producing during my years toiling away in restaurant kitchens. I had travelled the world making films, but I knew that there wasn't much further for me to go. I wasn't going to rise any further up the food chain, because I had ruffled too many feathers and hadn't played the political game. The game I did want to play, directing shoots, was itself changing: the shift from traditional film to digital cameras meant some of the old skills and tradecraft were dying out. Those on the up were more in the producer mould, a less creative, more bureau- cratic role. The business was changing and I just wasn't enjoying it as much as I had before.

The nadir came when I was packed off back to Birmingham to help staff a new diversity unit the BBC had established to get more non-white faces on screen. I was pretty well known by then as one of a few black direc- tors, and from their standpoint it seemed a natural fit. It soon became clear that this would be one of the worst experiences of my professional life. It was what I imagined working for the civil service would be like: very political, everything forensically checked for its potential to offend, most people frankly terrified to do anything at all. The whole enterprise was cloaked in nervousness and com- pletely lacking in any jeopardy. It was a political exercise, not a creative one, and that dictated the entire culture. It could not have been a worse fit for me.

With my television career becalmed, I had reached a dif- ficult moment. There was no jeopardy or excitement in it anymore, just the prospect of more of the same, at best. For me, it wasn't an option to keep going the way I was. The road ahead of me had run out, and the jeopardy lay in a change of course. It was around this very moment that something changed in my life. I met my wife, and within three months we were married. What had threatened to become a rut in my life became an exhilarating time when I felt that anything was possible. This is what motivated me to take what was probably the biggest risk of my life so far. The biggest because, by that stage, I finally had something to lose.

The short story is that we went into business together, co-founding a marketing agency for food and drink brands, Commsplus. It sounds simple enough, but for us both it was a real exercise in jeopardy. I had never so much as set foot through the doors of a PR or marketing company before, though my wife made up for that with a successful career in the industry behind her. More pressingly, when I left the BBC we had between us only enough money to pay the mortgage on our house for three months. I was going to have to learn an entirely new game and there wasn't much time to waste, or any real margin for error.

Yet I was much happier in the seemingly risky situation I was entering than in the one I was leaving, where I had comfort and security, but no real challenge or opportunity to grow. When you are starting something from scratch, with an immediate economic necessity to succeed, you are entering a phase of jeopardy that sharpens your focus: you don't waste time because you haven't got it to spare. Whether or not you succeed, you learn new things about yourself and extend the boundaries of what you are capable of.

It was a risk, but one I knew I had to take to avoid letting my dream peter out. The idea of owning a farm still burned within me, and while everything I had done at the BBC had moved me a hell of a lot closer to that than I had been a decade previously, I was still a long way from being in a position to become a landowner. I needed to make money, and I wasn't going to do that in any serious way as a job-bing television director. And if I wasn't going to become the boss in someone else's organisation, I knew the only choice was to become my own.

In the end, most of us have moments in our lives when there is a chance to change course, to do something differ-ent and to seize an opportunity that may not come around again soon, or indeed ever. Marriage to a brilliant woman and the tapering off of my television career offered one such moment. It was the closing of one path just as another began to reveal itself. For me, it became a simple choice, but the truth is that these chances are always cloaked in jeopardy, which is why many people opt not to take them.

You have to decide, for you, what is the greater risk? Would it be worse to try and possibly fail, or to stay forever on the treadmill you are already on? Both carry risks: on the one hand you might fail, get hurt and lose things that matter to you; on the other, you may become consumed with frustration about a job or career path you are no longer interested in. The greatest fallacy of all is that there is a choice without risk, a place of total safety and comfort to inhabit. There isn't; there are losses and gains either way and all of life is a risk. The question you must ask yourself is which path you want to take. But if you want excitement, achievement and fulfilment, that is going to mean choos-ing the path with jeopardy.

Getting noticed

Entering the marketing world and working with businesses for the first time, I learned a lot about how people perceive risk in the professional sphere. To cut a long story short, they see it everywhere: lurking around every corner, surrounding every opportunity and stalking every move they might conceivably make. The idea that something could go wrong weighs down every meeting and affects every decision. The constant question is not what do we stand to gain, but what might we end up losing? If there is one thing holding back many, many businesses in this country, it is the pervasive and deadening attitude to risk. You can see it in a lot of the language of business today: not plain and direct, but wrapped up in all sorts of crap jargon, obfuscation and, frankly, complete nonsense. It all comes from the same place: the desire to protect and hedge against the threat of disaster. Don't do anything that could come back to haunt us, don't try something that might fail, don't – whatever you do – say what you actually mean!

This tendency to focus on the wrong things extends to the corporate obsession with profit and the next quarter's financial results. Companies with such a narrow, short-term focus are only ever going to trip themselves up at some point, because they aren't doing the two things every good business should be doing: focusing on customers and embracing change. If you look at the food industry, the recent scandals are the result of producers prioritising not customers, quality and choice, but price, efficiency and convenience. They are thinking only of their profit margin, which clouds their view of what is really important, and ultimately encourages bad practices to develop. I think we are reaching a stage where we will start to see this corporate model change, the need for profit becoming better aligned with the needs of the customer for choice and quality, but we still have a long way to go.

All this fear of risk is true, in my experience, when you are talking about larger corporations. But there is another breed of businesses, one that thrives on risk as a necessary fuel for survival and growth. These are the entrepreneurial businesses, often young companies that can only make progress by being bold, standing out and casting aside the shackles that affect so many big companies. With my one experience of a corporate environment at the BBC, I knew that I could not seriously hope to work effectively with these monoliths. They wouldn't want to hear what I had to say, let alone act on it, and I was just going to get frustrated by my inability to make a dent on their approach to doing business.

At the outset of running Commsplus, I made a decision: we would seek to work only for brands in which we saw a bit of ourselves. Those who were outsiders, hungry for success, determined to try new things. People whose attitude to risk and appetite for jeopardy matched our own. So we sought and won business with young challenger brands, many of which are now familiar names, but were then in the early days of trying to shake up their markets. They included Cobra Beer, Loyd Grossman sauces, Kettle Chips and Plymouth Gin. We also did the PR for some famous chefs, including Raymond Blanc.

The years running that business were a great education for me, and I learned a lot about both my own appetite for risk and that of others. I wanted to do work that pushed the boundaries of what people expected and what might even be deemed acceptable. Instinctively, I knew that you need to take people to the edge, while being careful not to tip them over it – something that I put to good use when later starting The Black Farmer. You need would-be customers to be intrigued, but not indignant. Of course, some people will be offended whatever you do, but it is the majority that should concern you.

We did some quite maverick work that delivered against the need to raise the profile of our clients, often young or niche brands fighting for attention. With Plymouth Gin, we came up with the idea that they would 'sponsor' the 1999 solar eclipse, the first such event over mainland Britain in more than seventy years and expected to be at its most visible in the West Country. This was a brand whose only real differentiator was its place of origin, so we decided to play on that and to hitch our wagon to an event that was getting global attention. When we launched our poster campaign declaring Plymouth Gin sponsors of the eclipse, some people said, 'You can't do that', but my view was that there were no rules to be broken. Does the sun have image rights? It was a bit daring, but ultimately just a good joke that people took in the right spirit, and it worked as we had hoped.

With Mr Brain's, another client, we had the task of pop-ularising a very old dish that had, to say the least, fallen out of fashion. There isn't much you can do to glamourise a pork faggot, which is ultimately nothing more than mashed-up pig offal, but we had a go – if not at glamour, then at least at renewed acclaim. Our solution was to run a competition that sought to find the hidden champions of this forgotten dish: Britain's Faggot Family. Perhaps we were sailing a bit closer to the wind with that one, but it raised a huge amount of attention in the media; the winners even ended up on *The Graham Norton Show*, and sales went through the roof.

Both those campaigns, and the many others we ran, could easily have been nipped in the bud as unacceptable risks. Had they been presented to larger, more established brands, they would almost certainly have been. But in the end, if you are marketing a brand it is hard to get attention unless you ruffle a few feathers. That doesn't mean you should set out to offend or anger people, because of course they are the very consumers whose support you are seeking. But you do need an edge – a reason for people to engage with you and consider buying from you. Something which announces your intention to the market and speaks about the kind of brand you want to be. An expression of whose side you are on.

It is very hard to have edge without risking some kind of negative response. And that is what makes the larger brands flee in fear from anything that might do that. They focus to excess on what might upset a few people, not properly considering that there might be many more whose attention or support has been enlisted by the very same gambit. That, of course, was the philosophy behind the Black Farmer name. As I will explain, it generated some negative

feedback. But that was drowned out by the positive attention and consideration it garnered. The risk would have
been much greater had we chosen a bland name that had
struggled to get traction. Instead, by opting for something
bold, we actually minimised the greatest risk, which was
that no one would pay any attention to us at all. The path
of jeopardy was the one that paid off.

With Commsplus, though we worked for some brilliant
clients who were prepared to back bold visions, in the end
there were many more who wanted to water down plans
in search of what they deemed the more sensible option.
Good marketing cannot happen by committee, and big
ideas lose their edge when they are made safe for the corporate touch. There are only so many times you can put
up with marketing directors who are clearly acting in the
interests of their careers – and what they think their boss
will think – rather than doing what is needed to push a
brand forward. Creating the business had been an opportunity to be our own bosses, but in a service industry like
marketing you are never really the boss in everything you
do. Just like with the BBC, I was starting to see how the
corporate world wasn't really a meritocracy where you succeed on talent and ideas, but one where you had to learn
to survive the political game.

It was when we repitched for a piece of business, for a
company whom we had helped add thirty per cent to the
sales figures, that I realised I'd had enough. Our previous
work counted for nothing as we, in our forties, outlined
our vision to a group of twenty-somethings who obviously
thought they knew better. Our track record was cast to

one side, and safe to say we did not succeed. At that point I knew, just as I had before leaving the BBC, that I had to get out. Once again, the opportunity to seek out jeopardy and self-improvement had started to close down. Moreover, after almost a decade helping others to build their food brands, I was starting to feel ready to launch my own.

Picking fights

Almost everything about launching a business is a risk. You put your money, your reputation, maybe even your house on the line. You risk the safety and security of whatever job you are leaving behind. You risk the goodwill of family and friends whose needs you will ignore as you focus entirely on your business. Most of all, you risk that nobody will pay any attention to you whatsoever. The starting point of any enterprise is total invisibility. The brand exists only inside the heads of those who are creating it. What will determine its success is whether you can get anyone else to care about it. And some never get that far: the product or service might not be right, the timing could be wrong. There are so many reasons for failure, but some companies are doomed to remain as invisible when they die as they were at the moment of conception.

To shake off that cloak of invisibility, you have to be prepared to take risks. The biggest we took was our choice of name: The Black Farmer. As I have already explained, it tested badly in market research. We were told it would offend some people. And it did. I had people writing to me, saying that it was a racist statement. We had people getting in touch with the Commission for Racial Equality about us. When we launched our bacon with the packet promise of 'no shrinking, no white bits', we had more letters about our apparent racism.

Yet by generating interest and conversation, the name served its purpose. It had made us visible, the first step in the very difficult business of getting consumers to change their habits and buy a new food product. There are all sorts of reasons people buy what they do, and price is of course prominent among them, but loyalty is hugely important too. Consumers like what they have always liked; sometimes even the same things their parents used to buy. We are creatures of habit first and foremost, so getting someone to see something new, pick it up, consider it, buy it, take it home, cook it, eat it and then buy it again is some feat. And you will never get anywhere unless you persuade people to pick up your product and have a look in the first place.

The Black Farmer brand may have been our first and greatest risk, but a bold and edgy name will only take you so far. You cannot expect one risky move to be enough to build a business or career; you have to keep making them, to keep pushing boundaries and challenging people's expectations. As an entrepreneur, you also have to accept that success is about more than the risks you yourself take; it is also about who you can get to take a risk on you. Any business lives and dies on the support of customers, investors, suppliers and stakeholders. As a new company starting out, you have little else to offer other than the promise of your idea. You are asking people to buy into your vision and back it, to take a risk with you.

In the early days, we had both success and failure on this front. Before launch, when trying to raise money for the business, I came up against a brick wall with the banks. I learned the eternal lesson about finance, which is that money goes to those who already have it, and to people who look and sound like those who control it. As a black man going to talk to bank managers about farming and a food business, I met with total bemusement. I didn't fit into any neat and tidy box, or fulfil any stereotype. They frankly didn't know what to do with me, except to say that they couldn't help. In the end, the only loans I could get were by putting down a personal guarantee, risking everything I had, including my house. That is something a lot of entrepreneurs will have experienced and is, in itself, a good test of whether you really have an appetite for the task ahead. A lot of people will be telling you not to risk it and if you are wavering, you should question whether you actually have the commitment and the guts to see it through.

With the bankers, there was an easy way around their indifference, even if it did mean taking a big financial risk. But when it came to supermarket buyers, there was no room for failure. As a young food brand, you stand or fall on whether you can get the big retailers to buy into you. And as anyone who has ever tried to sell to supermarkets will tell you, it is a bloody nightmare. It took me back to my days of calling TV producers listed in the *Radio Times*. A lot of effort and not much in the way of immediate reward.

It goes a bit like this. If you can get a meeting in the first place, it will take forever to arrange; also expect to be mucked around on timing, to have appointments cancelled at the last minute, and to be kept waiting in reception for what feels like an age, amongst a group of fellow unfortunates who are engaged in the same nonsense. It is a slow torture when you arrive for a meeting that could make or break your business, to be sitting for up to an hour in a holding area, staring at the clock and pondering your fate. Be in no doubt that you are being kept waiting for a reason: to remind you of who is in charge, and of your place in the food chain.

I should say that, in my years running The Black Farmer, I have had the benefit of working with many excellent, personable and forward-thinking buyers who have been central to helping us on our journey. But there can be no denying that it is a forbidding experience for someone taking their first steps as a food entrepreneur. And in the early days, it proved a dispiriting one. I had really designed our product with Waitrose in mind, presenting our brand as a premium challenger to existing sausage brands, but they were not interested (and, funnily enough, our first listing ended up being with Asda). There was no luck with any of the other buyers I managed to get through to at that point, either.

I knew I needed a breakthrough, and I was not convinced that it was simply a matter of more phone calls and meetings until someone finally gave in. I could have wasted what time and money I had on this fool's errand, without the leverage I needed to broker a deal. So I took another big risk. I decided to take these people on and to hit them where it really mattered: with their customers.

A large part of our early strategy was to build local

awareness by displaying the brand and doing samplings at food and county shows. So we went all over the place with our stand and our sausages; good, old fashioned, face-to-face marketing. But after my discouraging experiences with supermarket buyers, I started to use these early customer encounters for something more than getting people to try the sausages. If you like the product, I said to them, do me a favour and tell the supermarkets they need to stock it. I had a website set up which listed the names and contact information of all the main supermarket sausage buyers. And I pointed people to it and asked them to make their voices heard.

That could have been a very stupid thing to do. I was harnessing the power of the customer voice – the one thing I knew the retailers actually feared – but doing so in a way that could easily antagonise the very people whose favour I was trying to win. All logic and common sense says that you need to make friends with these people. When they have a ready queue of supplicants willing to do anything to please them, why on earth would you risk getting in their bad books? The simple truth is that I knew what I had been trying wasn't working. Being polite and respectful was not getting me very far. So, again, the balance of risk had shifted. It posed a greater danger to my long-term prospects to keep doing the same thing again, rather than attempting a bold play that carried a great deal of jeopardy in its own right.

Again, I was pushing right to the edge, and I felt I had to: everything about that business was vested in getting a critical mass of listings with supermarkets that could deliver consumers at scale. There was no other way to win, so I took the risk of picking a fight with the retailers in order to get their attention. And it worked, because the first listing came off the back of that campaign, and more were to follow. I had, by force and through risk, opened the door that had at one point seemed stubbornly closed to me. The real trick was that it altered the risk calculation as far as would-be buyers were concerned. With customers advocating for me, suddenly the retailers had something to lose by not listing us, whereas before it had been all downside risk in taking a punt on an unknown quantity. By introducing some jeopardy into their thought process, we disrupted the party line that had prevailed in the initial meetings, and tipped the balance in our favour. My lesson there was that sometimes you need to introduce jeopardy into other people's lives if you are to get your way.

This wasn't a one off. I did a lot of things that other suppliers would have been terrified to do for fear of getting blacklisted. Most notably, I did a monthly column for a trade magazine, detailing my often frustrating experiences at the hands of the supermarket buyers: exposing the frequent lack of common courtesy, and calling out some of their more questionable practices. It got me noticed by some bigwigs, and I will name one supermarket here that did something as a result, for two reasons: firstly because I was impressed that they gave me the time of day as a small, barely established supplier; and secondly, because I'd rather they didn't delist me now! It was Sainsbury's who invited me in for a meeting with their then boss, Justin King, and Mike Coupe, who has since taken over from him.

They have taken a lead in showing willingness to engage with smaller suppliers, and others would do well to follow that example.

In the end, I think I forged better relationships because I took a risk that went against what retailers expected from prospective suppliers. I made my case and I wasn't shy about letting plenty of people hear it. It could easily have backfired or been turned against me, but in the end it proved to be in my favour.

And that is the crucial thing: you often won't know whether something you are about to try is going to work. Some risks do not pay off and some really blow up in your face. The important thing is to be free enough to make a mistake. You have to be able to afford for things to go wrong, and to create some space to allow you to be daring. That margin for error may be small, but you will need it all the same, because in the end when you are building a business, it effectively comes down to the risks you take and those that others take on you. No one is going to bet the farm on someone who is themselves paralysed by caution. To find other risk-takers, you need to show some intent of your own. And you have to be prepared for it all to go wrong, before you can expect to see a few things start to go right.

CHAPTER 9

Seek out adversity

A lot of entrepreneurs talk about being driven by hunger, but I can remember what it is like to actually be hungry – having to crunch chicken bones between my teeth because that was sometimes all we had. When you are hungry the next meal becomes like an obsession, and you treat it with something approaching reverence. One mealtime for which we would never go short was Sunday lunch, when by tradition we would enjoy my mother's version of the Caribbean national dish, jerk chicken with rice and peas. Poor we might have been, but I always felt like a king with this feast in front of me. Much more often, however, it was a case of sharing what little we had among the many mouths around the table that needed feeding. In those circumstances, you learned that nothing gets thrown away.

What the poverty of my childhood also taught me is that adversity is one of the constant features of life, and there is nothing you can do to escape it. In my case, it was something my family experienced a lot of – from our economic circumstances to the colour of our skin in 1960s and '70s Britain. I learned early on in life that you can't expect to have things handed to you, and that you have to fight for the things you want. As a poor, black, dyslexic kid, told he was stupid by teachers and that he would never amount to anything, I discovered that nobody is going to make your dreams happen for you, and in fact many more are likely to stand in your way than help you.

But adversity is not the sole preserve of those who get a bad deal in life's lottery. Of course, you are going to have a tougher time if you are born poor. But you can be wealthy, accepted, with every possible advantage in life too. There are still very few lives that go untouched by adversity. Bad things happen to us all, rich and poor, black and white, privileged and outcast. To succeed we must all learn not just to cope with adversity, but to make the very best out of it. And if you are going to follow the advice in this book and embrace jeopardy, then you need to get used to adversity not just as an occasional guest in your life, but as a permanent fellow traveller.

We have just talked about risk, and how it is your attitude towards it that matters most of all. The same is ultimately true with adversity, but the reality is much starker. The misfortunes that befall us all are not something you can prepare for or weigh carefully in advance. There is no range of options to choose from in terms of how bad things are going to be. They just happen, arriving suddenly and unexpectedly, in your personal or professional life. People we care about die. Work we depend upon goes away. You might get seriously ill, as happened to me a few years ago.

Or you might do something stupid that puts you or other people in danger. Often there is no rhyme or reason, no responsibility attached, no blame to be apportioned. Our misfortunes can be as senseless as they are sudden, but that does not take away the reality of having to deal with them.

And deal with them you must, because there is no problem greater than one ignored or suppressed. The people who end up suffering the most are those who spend their whole lives trying to avoid pain, because when adversity finally gets past their defences – and it will – then they have nothing left to shield themselves with. They have not built up the inner strength needed to accept it and keep on going. There is some of the logic of inoculation that applies here. A little bit of what you fear can go a long way to helping protect you against worse things to come.

Your experiences are your armour in life; those who have gone through adversity know that their difficulties were often not as bad as they initially seemed. And there is no greater shield than knowing you have survived something worse than the issue currently facing you. If, like me, you have come from society's dustbin heap and made something of yourself, then you know you can survive whatever obstacles are placed in your path. It gives you a strength and sense of validation that nothing else can.

This is why we must embrace jeopardy and accept adversity into our lives. It makes us stronger, more enduring and better prepared for the challenges that lie ahead. It is a form of life training essentially no different from an athlete putting in miles on the track, or a surgeon spending hours in the operating theatre. Adversity is not just an inescapable part of all our lives, but also the most important preparation there is for living the life you want and pursuing your dream. For it is the lessons learned and the strength developed in our toughest times that give us the motivation and means to push ourselves forward to better days.

Overcoming the worst

Our immediate, instinctive reaction to adversity is to protect ourselves. Defence mechanisms kick in: how do we shield ourselves from the threat of harm? This survivor's mentality is natural enough, but it is actually counterproductive to your long-term interests. And it is something you must learn to curb if you really want to achieve your dreams in life.

Adversity is one of life's most important teachers, and it has two great lessons to impart. The first is that you can survive the worst life has to throw at you. When you have dealt with adversity, such as losing the people you love, being kicked out of your job, overcoming disability or illness, then you are a stronger person for it. It is hard, sometimes horribly so, but there is a strength to be drawn from the knowledge that you made it through, you were not beaten and you have lived to fight another day. Adversity teaches us about ourselves: what we are capable of, how we react to situations, our best and worst traits. It gives you self-awareness and a deeper knowledge of the person and character you really are.

Adversity's second great lesson is about itself: that it will always be there, whether present in your life or lurking in the background. When you have had to fight to take one step towards your dream, you know that none of your ambitions is going to come easily, and that you will have to battle the whole way. I understood at a young age that everything I wanted to achieve in life was going to be met by adversity. Getting into the BBC, setting up my first business, buying the farm, raising money for The Black Farmer, standing for Parliament, surviving leukae- mia. Every one of those things was against the odds, and every one of them came with closed doors that had to be forced open or worked around. But I was ready for those obstacles, because I never went into a single one of those ventures thinking that it would be easy, that the door would be held open, or a path cleared for me. I always knew I had to cut my own path and find my own way. The adversity of my early life conditioned me to do what was necessary to succeed.

When you know that life is bloody tough, and that nothing worthwhile is ever going to be easy, you put your- self in a better position to start achieving the things you want. The recognition that the road towards your dreams is littered with hazards is one of the best ways to prepare for facing them. With that knowledge, you are not only forewarned but forearmed, with an essential confidence in your own ability to overcome the worst.

It's no coincidence that some of the world's most success- ful people have lives which were marked by real adversity, in childhood or early career. Oprah Winfrey, who became one of the most prominent media and public figures of her generation, began life in rural poverty and was sexually abused by members of her own family. She is today, according to several rankings, the most influential woman in the world. Benjamin Franklin, arguably the greatest inventor of all time, was one of seventeen children, and his formal education ended at the age of ten. Largely self-taught, he went on to become one of the most important thinkers of his or any age, not to mention his role as a Founding Father of the United States.

The list could go on. I can guarantee that almost anyone whose success you admire has, in their personal or professional life, gone through some kind of adversity. They might have overcome poverty, abuse or addiction growing up, or had to deal with the setbacks that affect many ambitious people when they are starting out. Most successful business people have failed at one point or another. Most brilliant artists have gone through a period of being unrecognised. Some of the greatest athletes were at one point or other told that they were never going to make it. And many of them will turn around and say that it was the best thing that ever happened to them; that the things they learned about themselves and about life gave them the essential strength needed to achieve their dreams and conquer the world.

In the end, you need adversity because it toughens you up. And it gives you one more, precious thing. Motivation. There is nothing like adversity for fanning the flame of a dream into a burning fire within you. When you have suffered, been told that you are not good enough and that it is never going to happen, you go one of two ways. Either you accept your lot in life, or you fight against it. And if you are someone who chooses to fight, then you have a mission that is unlike any other. You are battling not just to fulfil a dream, but to prove others wrong. And there is no more powerful motivation than that.

Making life harder

The question you must ask yourself is not 'will I face adversity?', but *'how* will I face it?' For it is in all our lives; if not now, then almost certainly lying in wait. It could be something big or small, something you had thought about or an event that is entirely unexpected. It might be a problem you have helped to cause, or something for which you are entirely blameless. Whatever the case may be, it is your response to adversity that defines you. And there are really only two ways a person can go.

The first is to run away from the problem, to be in denial, to try and ignore the consequences. Whether that is something as simple as a mistake at work or as serious as losing your job, there is ample scope for self-justification and self-pity. This might feel good, but it is not going to help you. There are people who spend their whole lives trying to escape their problems and to deny the possibility that they have the power to make things better. If you want it to be so, there can always be some external force or being to blame, always someone else who is stopping you from achieving what you want in life.

The other road is to run towards the problem, taking responsibility for dealing with a situation, whether or not you are the one responsible for creating it. If you are given a hard lot in life, do you bemoan your circumstances, or do you make it your personal mission to escape them? I know plenty of people from my childhood who have ended up on both sides of that divide; some who made poverty their reason to fail and others who have harnessed it as the absolute motivation to succeed. I'm not pretending it is easy to defy your circumstances or the box that society seeks to put you in. But it is possible. It can be done. I am, along with many others, living testament to that. To do so requires a positive attitude towards adversity, one that lets you use it to your advantage and learn the lessons it has to teach.

That very same mindset is the one that people from all walks of life will need in order to face the mishaps, great and small, that affect us all. If you have messed up for some reason, then admit to it, own the mistake and show what you are going to do to rectify it. The thing to be ashamed of is not failing in the first place, but a failure to be honest about what has happened and a failure to learn for the future. If something terrible happens in your life, then you are going to need some time to try and understand it: what happened, why did it happen, what does it mean? But the best response is to ask another question: what do I do now? This means not being the victim of events, but taking back control over them. In even the most difficult of circumstances, there is comfort to be taken, there are lessons to be learned and opportunities to make positive resolutions about the future. We are not what our circumstances make us, but what we make of them.

Adversity is a clarifying force in our lives. It strips away the noise that surrounds us and lets us focus on the things that matter most. It is an opportunity to reassess who we are, the things we do and those we still want to achieve. You can use it either as a fundamentally positive moment to make changes in your life that will help you move towards your dream; or you can let it be a damaging headwind that blows you off course. The important thing to remember is that the choice is yours. You might not have had agency over what happened to you, but no one can take away your power to respond to it. You can't change what happened, but you can shape what happens next.

In fact, I think adversity is so important in the shaping of our characters and in the achievement of our dreams that I believe people should actively seek it out. Now I'm not saying go out and break a leg, throw away all your money or hope something really bad happens. But there are all sorts of ways in which we can challenge ourselves with what I would call small doses of everyday adversity; situations that will challenge us, demanding that we respond and learn. That could be volunteering to take on a new role at work or to do something you would not normally do, such as public speaking or a presentation. Ideally, it should be something you don't relish the prospect of or necessarily think you can do. By pushing yourself into uncomfortable situations, you learn new things about yourself. Often you will be surprised by what you can do when you are given no option but to have a go. It could even be something as small as deciding to learn a new language or develop a new skill – anything that stretches you, makes you feel a bit uncomfortable and helps you to learn. Because we do not get better by doing the things we already do well. We have to get out of the comfort zone, feel the threat of failure hanging over us, create a little bit of adversity for ourselves to fight against. It is by embracing jeopardy that we develop the confidence, the techniques and the resolve to overcome adversity. We have to step further than we think is possible before we can start to get anywhere at all.

Learning from setbacks

Preparation for adversity is essential, because if you are chasing a big dream, then you are going to face plenty of it, at every stage. Perhaps this is no more true than when you are starting out, taking your first steps on that journey, standing at the bottom of the mountain and wondering how the hell you are going to climb it.

One of the realities of life is that good ideas get passed over and good people get rejected. Consider some of the most successful novelists of our generation, from J.K. Rowling to Stephen King, who were turned down by multiple publishers before they finally found an opening. Being rejected is not necessarily a judgement on you. It doesn't mean that you or your idea are crap. It just means that you have not yet struck upon the right person, at the right time, in the right frame of mind.

Rejection is the first and most obvious form of adversity that we will all face, whether our dreams are in business, the arts, science or sport. No one gets the thumbs up from every examiner or interviewer. And everyone must learn to cope with being told that they haven't been successful, in a job application, a sales pitch, or an audition of any kind. In fact, it is far better if you experience at least a little rejection before you get your breakthrough. Because then you are battle-hardened for all the challenges that are to come. You know what it is like for things to go wrong, and how you can start to set about making them right.

To illustrate, let me take you back to the very earliest days of my venture into the food business. This was a year or two before I launched The Black Farmer, and even before I knew that I would make sausages my launch product. I had not long since completed the refurbishment of my farm and purchased my first flock of sheep. I was convinced of two things: the first was that British lamb was the best in the world, and that other people needed to know it; the second was that other sheep farmers were getting it wrong by selling their meat at knockdown prices to distributors. Surely, I thought, there was a gap in the market to sell direct to consumers, who could know they were getting Black Farmer lamb, reared with love and care, and the best that money could buy.

So I set myself up with a website, some smart packaging and expensive branded carrier bags. I let all my family and friends know it was coming and told them to spread the word. And I decided to road test my new venture by slaughtering just one lamb. My excitement quickly turned to frustration once I got down to the selling. Because there are many different parts of the animal you can eat, but seemingly only one that any customers wanted to buy. Perhaps the shoulder? No, just chops. Or a crown? Chops. Surely you'd like a leg, the king of roasts? Chops again. I could have sold lamb chops all day long, but the problem was that I couldn't sell anything else. And I tell you, the rest of that carcass sat in pieces in my freezer for six months, as family and friends got for free the cuts I had wanted to make a business out of selling. With the remainder of the sheep, I ended up resorting to doing exactly what I had chided my peers for doing: selling on the cheap to a distributor. I was a farmer at last, and starting to learn why some had warned me how hard it would be.

It's hard to understate what a chastening experience that was. Remember that owning a farm had been my dream for decades. And now, in my first real venture as a farmer, I had been met with resounding defeat, a failure I was literally made to chew on for months afterwards, ruining the taste of much excellent lamb. Yet I learned from that failure, and the lesson was perhaps the most fundamental one there is in business. You must give the customer what they want. That doesn't mean there is no scope for innovation and change, but unless you are tapping into something that is already there, as we did with gluten-free products, then you will fail. Consumer preference cannot be created through force of will or good marketing. You must meet the customer where they already are, or somewhere they have already thought of going.

There were virtues in my early thinking. Direct-to-consumer was the right idea, and when it came to launching The Black Farmer properly, sampling programmes played a big part in building the momentum to get supermarket listings. I was also right that consumers would respond to a brand that was personal and offered a stronger connection with the food you buy. But I had got one very important thing wrong, and that was what ultimately made the difference. When you fail, you have to be very honest with yourself: what did you do right and what did you get wrong? The natural response is to say that failure means you were entirely misguided, and to write off your entire strategy, when that is probably not the appropriate response. It may just be, as with my unfortunate sheep, there was too much of what people didn't want, even though there were some things they did. The adversity of failure presents an opportunity to reassess, and to filter the good from the bad. Most early-stage propositions are a mixture of the two; future success depends on sorting the one from the other, and working out how to focus on the winning ingredients. Only by getting it wrong do you actually learn how the reality stacks up against your expectations, giving you the evidence you need to make adjustments and try again.

So I learned from that difficult experience, and when it came to launching the business for real, I focused on the sausage, something I knew British consumers already loved. That removed one of the obstacles in our way: we knew there was no question of whether people wanted to buy them. Our task then became convincing people – retailers and consumers alike – that ours were the sausages for them, a much easier conversation than trying to convince someone to try a product they do not have any initial interest in. The same basic premise has been our guide as we have expanded the range of Black Farmer products over the years, from the traditional banger to a wide variety of sausages, plus eggs, bacon, roasting joints, burgers, meatballs, chicken pieces and cheddar. Just don't talk to me about lamb chops!

Sticking to your guns

Just as getting a career off the ground is often the hardest part, most entrepreneurs will face real challenges in the early days of their business: in both cases it's about getting your foot in the door, and that can be a foreboding and frustrating process. But don't expect the fun to stop there. Oh no, your troubles are only just beginning. You have made it to the starting line, and an entire obstacle course awaits you, for as long as you choose to tackle it.

Like any business, we have faced plenty of adverse moments in building The Black Farmer into a recognised brand. Of course there were the fundamental difficulties, as I have discussed already, about getting our big break-through and being noticed by the right people in order to succeed, but below that were also a sea of annoying details and unexpected events, threatening to trip us up on almost every day of being in business.

If I think back to getting the product into supermarkets, we faced an almost bizarre battle of wills about whether the product was suitable for this or that audience. I was always proud of our status as a West Country product, but equally determined that we had the appeal and distinctiveness to reach a national audience. Not everyone shared that view, but they could not even agree on what they disagreed on. At different stages, I had local sourcing managers telling me that the product was not local enough, while national buyers told me that it was too regional for them. At that point, your head does start to spin a little.

It did not prove an insurmountable hurdle, but there was soon another obstacle rushing towards us. You might reasonably think that getting into the supermarkets is the hardest job, and in some ways this is true. However, once you are over the threshold, you have entered a lion's den of negotiation and browbeating. This is the battle for margin, in which every inch is fought over as if a matter of life and death. In this business, no scrap of success goes unpunished: start selling well and a retailer might offer you increased volume, but they're going to want something for it, and – you guessed – it's a bigger slice of your precious profit margin. It doesn't end there, either, because the moment you have given one retailer a better deal, be sure that their competitors will find out and be on the phone demanding something even more favourable to guarantee their ongoing support. It's an experience I have likened to being a mere mortal, with the gods of retail on their Mount Olympus, chucking down lightning bolts at your fragile vessel of a brand.

Sometimes it's not you that these deities choose to visit their wrath upon, but each other. While running The Black Farmer, I have found myself closer to combat zones than I ever did during my year in the military. It usually goes a bit like this: summer approaches, the weather gets warmer, and with barbeque season in mind, the sausage category starts to become a key battlefield. Very quickly, a smaller player like us can find ourselves in the middle of a price war as the big boys load up their bazookas with price promotions, pitting their premium brands against each other. This is an approach we can never hope to compete with. Without trashing our margin or our quality, there is very little we can directly do to compete. Very little, that is, except to fall back on the one advantage we have: customer loyalty to the brand.

In business, you have to be keenly aware of where you can and cannot compete. There is no point in trying to take on outsize opponents on a field of their choosing where they have all the advantages. That does not mean, however, that your fate is sealed. They might have the heavy equipment, but you are the guerrilla fighter with advantages they do not have, and an ability to go to places they cannot reach. When a battle is on and you fear the consequences, you must make sure to play to your own strengths and not to those of your competitors. We have survived these frequent price wars because we believe in the power of our brand, we continue to cultivate our customers and we never forget that there is more to food retail than price alone.

A lot of success over the long term is about sticking to your guns, even when the conditions appear to be adverse and suggest that a change of course would be logical. When you know you are right, and that you would have to compromise your vision to adapt, then that is the time to dig in and fight for what you believe in. In the case of Black Farmer sausages, my guiding star since the very first day has been the quality of the product: British pork and lots of it, with a high meat content unadulterated by the excessive amounts of water and alien additives that some producers bulk out their sausages with. We have always stood by the importance of a premium product, backed up by a brand that people can connect with and believe in. Yet there is jeopardy in having a model that is so inflexible, because the circumstances can change around you, as they have sometimes done with the cost of ingredients rising. This is one of the things that gives you sleepless nights when running a food business, and it is only ever so long before the nightmare arrives, and inflation reaches the point where you have no choice but to go cap in hand to your customers and request the one thing a retailer hates above all: a price rise.

My trick is to send the emails on a Friday, in the hope that proximity to the weekend will allow some time for the news to sink in, and for the buyers to calm down. A few days later I take a deep breath and pick up the phone to ring around my overlords. I will always remember the response of one buyer the first time I had to do this, who gave me the heartiest laugh down the phone, before telling me that they had a system in place to automatically delete supplier emails requesting a price rise. He was joking (though knowing retailers, he might not have been) and, to my much greater surprise, he was sympathetic to my plight. Indeed, most of the retailers on that occasion said that they too had been tracking the rising price of pork and were happy to support me. I need not have been so worried. I was proved right in sticking to my principles and doing what was the right thing for my business: maintaining the quality of the product and asking for a fair price. For while adversity has a huge amount to teach you about what you need to change and do better – whether that is as an individual or with your business – it also throws up circumstances when the best course is to keep going with what you know to be right. You must experience adversity and learn to use it to your advantage, but you cannot allow it to blow you off course and cloud your vision either.

Battle scars

Sometimes adversity strikes when you least expect it, and in ways you can never really prepare for. I thought that, with all my life experience, there was not much left to surprise me or trip me up. But then, in 2014 at the age of fifty-seven, I got ill. Or to be specific, I was diagnosed with a condition I had actually had, without realising it, for over fifteen years. That was myelofibrosis, a rare disease that affects your bone marrow. In my case, as can happen, it had turned into an acute form of leukaemia.

Those who have been in that situation themselves, or with a loved one, know what it feels like as the doctors start to talk in percentages, and it dawns on you that this is really serious. I could die. In fact I am probably going to. I was lucky, because if it had been a decade earlier then the science would not have been there to save me. As it was, with brilliant treatment, a stem-cell transplant and a year spent in hospital including some pretty close scrapes with the other side, I somehow survived.

Now, every time I look in the mirror I am reminded of what I went through, because the illness attacked my skin pigmentation, leaving me with vitiligo and patches all over my face, hands and body. It got my tastebuds too, leaving me unable to taste the sweet things I used to enjoy so much, although thankfully I can still taste the sausages. These battle scars are not something I regret or despise, however. Instead, they remind me of what I learned while sitting in the hospital bed, not sure if I was waiting to die or if I would ever make it back to my farm.

What I learned was, even at my age and with all my experience, I was still allowing things that didn't really matter to crowd out those that did; letting the clutter and noise of everyday life drown out the most important people and things. It was perhaps the greatest example I have known of adversity acting as a cleansing force, stripping away the irrelevant and the unimportant, and making me focus only on what really mattered. The imminent threat of death made very clear how much of my thinking had been white noise, irrelevant to the big picture. With all this spare time on my hands, I did something of a life audit in my head, reflecting on the things I had and hadn't done, and those I still wanted to do. How could I live my life better, if I was given that opportunity, run my businesses better, and be a better person for the people I most cared about?

Without doubt, since the illness I have been able to focus better on the really important things, because I know there is only so much time left, and I cannot afford to waste it. So whenever something comes up, I apply a very simple test: is it one of those important things and does it contribute to things I want to still be doing in a year's time? Is it something I actually want to do? And if the answer to either of those questions is no, then I don't do it.

So I am redoubling my efforts on the business, which funnily enough did even better when I was ill than it had before. We're doing what we have always done and trying to anticipate consumer tastes by creating an entire visitor experience on the farm, complete with restaurant, culinary training school and shop. It's the fulfilment of the vision I have always had for a brand that really allows people to feel a connection with the food and the farm. I've done some more frivolous things too, including following a long-time passion to take up flamenco dancing, buying myself a property in Spain as well as some pretty snazzy outfits. In fact that was one of the first things I did after breaking out of hospital. It might have seemed silly, but it was one of the things I had dreamed about stuck in that bed for a year, and I was determined not to waste a moment in making it happen. Illness has a habit of focusing the mind like that. You cast aside the things that suddenly no longer seem to matter, and you focus like hell on the things and people that really do.

Since the illness I think I have become a better person in so many ways: better at running my business, better at caring for my family, better at recognising the importance of the people around me. As I write this, I am hobbling around on crutches waiting for a hip operation, another bloody medical drama I didn't need. But again, as so often with these moments of adversity, there was a blessing hidden somewhere; it has brought home to me more than ever the kindness of people who ask if I need help, hold doors open for me and otherwise go out of their way to help someone who is struggling a bit. When we are healthy and focused only on our own ambitions and dreams, it is easy to go through life without noticing what you have around you. The adversity of illness is a great eye-opener: it makes you appreciate more what you have, and it gives you that extra hunger to achieve those things that are still left to be done.

We will all experience moments of adversity in life, whether they be misfortunes that befall us or those close to us; whether they are life-threatening or simply unsettling and hurtful. And we will all be shaped by this adversity and the opportunity for reflection, learning and self-awareness it creates, however hard that may seem. We all bear the scars that life leaves on us, but there can be good that comes from events that initially seem impossible and unjust. By making the decision to respond to adversity with a positive attitude, you can take a much bigger piece out of it than it does of you. With the vitiligo I suffered, I have various camouflaging make-up kits that I can use to hide the patches on my face, but I don't, and only partly because it is a pain to apply and remove the make-up; those scars mean something, and their presence serves a positive purpose. They are a reminder that I won that battle, and that I now feel better equipped than ever for the challenges that still lie ahead.

If you are a person who decides to live with jeopardy, then I can guarantee that you are going to encounter more than your fair share of adversity. I can also promise you that, strange as it might sound, this is something you will benefit greatly from. People who have come through and out the other side of adversity are almost always stronger for it. And by seeking out a life where challenges and difficulty are waiting for you at every turn, you will be giving yourself the best possible training and preparation to achieve your dreams in life.

CHAPTER 10

Keep the faith

The leap of faith. It's an essential component of a life lived with jeopardy and something you are going to have to take to achieve your dream. Nothing difficult or interesting has ever been done without someone having an essential belief in what they were trying to do, often going against the consensus view of the time. It is only with faith that we can do the things that change our lives and those of the people around us. The intrinsic jeopardy of any big dream is that we don't know if we will be good enough to achieve it, or if the idea itself will work. Only faith can help to overcome that deficit of certainty. You will never truly know until you have tried.

Starting a business is a leap of faith. Changing your job is a leap of faith. Falling in love and getting married is a leap of faith. Almost everything we can do in our lives that will change them for the better involves doing something where there is a good deal of jeopardy involved in the outcome. We don't know whether our idea will work, whether our skills will find their natural home with a new employer or how we will feel about the person we love today in five, ten, twenty years' time.

So much of life is about imperfect information – not knowing enough and having to do it anyway. The only way you can do that is with faith, and I deliberately use a word that would not usually be seen as appropriate in a professional context. If you went into a business meeting tomorrow and started talking about the importance of faith, you would probably get some strange looks in response. People start to think about blind faith, about trying things that have no evidence to back them up, but that is little more than the classic attempt to deny the reality of jeopardy and strip away the inevitable risk that will always be present in doing anything worthwhile. When making any big decision it's likely that you will have some evidence to go on, but plenty of gaps in your awareness. You will still have to act anyway, because timing is everything in life, and opportunities do not wait around for you to become perfectly informed. By the time you are, someone else will have acted where you did not, and the window will have closed.

Leaps of faith are necessary because we live in a competitive world in which you have to grab opportunities or watch someone else steal them away from you. If I had never taken a leap of faith, I would still be exactly where I had started out, Small Heath in Birmingham, living the same life as my parents did, doing one of the crap jobs that was foretold as my lot in life. Only through faith – by believing in my dream, in myself and converting others to the same cause – have I been able to achieve the things I have.

Faith matters because, without it, you are a fundamentally empty vessel. Faith is what gives you the inner
strength to overcome the adversity you will face in pursuing a dream; it is what you need to inspire in other people
to get your ideas off the ground.

Every inventor, every visionary business leader, every
pioneering scientist once had faith in something that was
ridiculed by almost everyone else. They saw the potential
in ideas that were written off as lunatic by supposedly
sensible people who were actually stuck in the status quo.
The only reason we can live today with supercomputers in
our pockets, connected to information and people across
the globe at the touch of a button, is because some crazy
people had faith that they could change the world. It may
be inner genius and intellectual agility that creates these
ideas, but it is faith above all that sees them made real. It
is faith that allows the germ of these big visions to become
incredible realities.

Faith is about more than just believing in yourself,
though that of course is hugely important. It is also the
basis on which you build a business, just as it has been the
foundation of religious movements down the centuries.
There are plenty of parallels. A movement starts with one
or a few true believers on their own, often isolated from
the mainstream. It grows through recruiting disciples, the
people who are going to work for you, buy from you and
invest in you. The message is carried through your apostles,
those people of influence who help to advance your cause
and attract more disciples. At the heart of it is a creed: an
idea to believe in, a sense that you have something new and

important to offer. Everyone involved is bound together by an essential faith: that they are doing something worthwhile, important, for the right reasons.

And if that might strike you as a touch blasphemous, then don't forget that religion is the oldest and biggest business in the world. According to Georgetown University, the total value of religion and associated activities in the United States is $1.2 trillion a year – more than the combined revenues of the ten largest American tech companies put together, including the likes of Apple, Google and Facebook. Faith sells. It always has, and it continues to do so, in the religious context and far beyond. You need to have faith – in yourself and your ideas – but if you really want to succeed then you also need to learn how to franchise it, to make others believe as much as you do.

Have faith in yourself

I do not belong to any particular church or religious community, but I would certainly describe myself as a man of faith. I have always had an inner belief in my ability to achieve the things I wanted. That belief is not just in myself; it is in the power of the individual to improve their life and change their circumstances, if they show the required passion and positive attitude. I believe everyone can do that, whether it is to escape a life they do not want to live, or to improve the one they already have. That is what this whole book is about.

If you are going to succeed in doing that, you need faith. In fact you will need to go on a whole journey of faith, from harnessing your own to inspiring that of other people. But it can only start in one place and that is with you. Faith in yourself is the foundation stone of any dream: you are never going to get close to achieving it unless you have that, for how can you expect anyone else to believe in you, if you do not have faith in your own ideas and capabilities?

This self-belief comes much easier for some people than others, but don't worry if you are not one of the those swaggering types who looks as if they are ready to conquer the world before they have had their morning Shreddies. Bluster and bullshit can conceal much more than it demonstrates, and often the people who flaunt it are seeking to make up for even greater insecurities than the person who seems to doubt themselves.

I am a pretty confident guy, but I have been through some very dark periods in my life when I really was not sure if I had what it took to succeed. I remember being at the BBC, working through the nights to write scripts – a task that my dyslexia made almost impossible – feeling terrified of being discovered and outed as a fraud. It is perfectly natural to doubt yourself, and in fact you will find that many people cite doubt as a central tenet of religious belief and philosophy. None of us is perfect or immune to the ravages of self-doubt. We all have flaws to overcome, gaps in our expertise and things we are simply not confident about doing. This is another one of those adversities we have just looked at, the things that can make you stronger when you survive them and live to tell the tale. It will often be people who have overcome their own doubts, and their self-confessed shortcomings, who come out with the strongest faith in their ability to succeed. When you know that you can do something that you once thought was beyond you, you are a much stronger person than the one who pretends and seeks to blag their way to victory.

So how do we gain this confidence in ourselves, this faith in our own abilities? The first thing is to focus on what you can already do well. It may be that there are some things you will never relish or be expert at. That is fine, because life is not a solo act; there are going to be other people on your journey, as partners, friends or employees who can make up for your shortcomings. But without a doubt, there will be things you *are* good at. So look at them, take the positive attitude to your strengths and weaknesses, and think about where those virtues could take you. What can you do well that others cannot? What makes you stand out? What one thing can you always rely on, however difficult the circumstances? Start from a point of confidence and strength, a faith in what you are already capable of.

The other obvious way to gain confidence is to try things out. You will often find that the thing you feared is simply not as bad as had been expected. Find low-risk ways to test yourself and discover that failure is not actually the last judgement that many consider it to be. Instead it is something you can learn from, and which helps you to get better and more confident. If we can laugh in the face of our fears and our doubts, suddenly they do not seem nearly as intimidating as they did when they were just an anonymous beast, yet to be encountered.

The beginning of establishing faith in yourself is getting confident about your abilities. But faith has to be external as well as internal. A big part of believing in yourself is about your ability to effect change. To defy conventions to make things happen. Faith cannot just be about waiting around for good things to happen, or doing the same thing over and again while expecting a different result – that is the blind faith of the gambler, always anticipating a big win around the corner if they only wait. Blind faith cannot help you, unless you get lucky. But a faith in yourself, in your ability to learn, get better and overcome the obstacles in your path; that is something you need and which will be one of your greatest allies.

The difference is that blind faith means a passive expectation that things will get better, while real faith is a belief that you yourself can make them better. A belief that you have the power to bend circumstances to your will and to create a path to the life you want to live. This is a faith that inspires you to take action, and which provides the sustenance you need when adversity strikes and you are not sure if you can carry on.

One the greatest challenges we have in our lives is overcoming the tendency to keep repeating our mistakes, whether that is at work or in our personal relationships. It is so easy to get caught in the trap of recreating the same circumstances, over and over again. Like being stuck in a bad film where you already know the ending. To break out of that cycle, and to pursue your dreams, you need to have that essential faith: both in your ability to change as a person, and in your capability to effect change around you. Then, and only then, can you hope to start winning the faith and support of the other people you will need.

Have faith in your ideas

Inside every dream there is an idea, whether that is to emulate someone whose life you admire, to solve a problem that has affected your life or to create something of value that you don't think yet exists. As I have already discussed, other people's default response to such ideas will be to dismiss them. You're not good enough. It's already being done. The market's too competitive. You haven't got a hope.

You will get used to hearing things like that, both from people who are well meaning and others who are not, so having faith in your idea, the guiding purpose for your dream in life, is second only in importance to having faith in yourself. The moment I learned this, more than any other, was when I finally achieved the dream I had nurtured since the age of eleven in my father's allotment, and became the proud owner of my farm. The moment I saw it, I fell in love. I knew after all those years that it was the place I had been waiting for my whole life. But if you are having visions of rolling fields, a rustic farmhouse and dry stone walls, let me disabuse you. This place I decided I must have was a real dump. No mains water (it had to be manually pumped in, daily), no sewage, no gas or central heating. Pretty derelict all round. It had been in the same family for some time, and they were just grateful to have it off their hands. It did not look like the sunlit uplands of a dream I had been holding in my heart for decades. All the farm buildings were in need of urgent repair, and it was going to cost me almost everything I had to rebuild the place from top to bottom. But it had the potential. It was a place that needed some passion put into it, a place that needed rescuing.

I saw the fulfilment of my idea, the realisation of my dream, in a broken-down bit of old farmland that would have sent most people running for the hills, with good reason. That for me sums up a very important point: these ideas, these opportunities that come along in life, are what we as individuals make of them. We do not all see the same things when we look at the same picture. Some might see things that terrify or disgust them. Others might find wonder. And if you are seeing an opportunity in something that others have discounted, then don't let them stop you from taking it seriously. Of course you must think properly about it, because sometimes we all have flights of fancy that don't work out. But if you are convinced, if you have faith that something can be achieved, then the fact that others doubt you is not a good enough reason to stop pursuing the idea.

When I bought that farm and resolved to turn it into the place I had always dreamed of, it wasn't just the renovation that posed a challenge. It was the entire farming industry and sector of the economy that I was seeking to join. I had bought a small dairy farm, something that is a major plank of Britain's agricultural economy, but one that has been struggling for many years. For the townies among you reading this, the real price of the cheap milk you can buy in the supermarket is that it is putting dairy farmers out of business. The margins are so tight, and the retailers so reluctant to make prices reasonable on such a

staple product, that it has become a life and death struggle for most small producers. To give you an idea, in the
late 1990s, when I bought my little farm, there were over
30,000 dairy farm holdings in the UK. The total number
today is less than half of what it was then.

When I bought the farm, most people could see the way
the wind was blowing and were looking to get out of the
business before it bankrupted them. So I was really going
against the grain in almost every conceivable way: as a black
man trying to become a farmer in the south-west, buying a
property that needed a complete overhaul and entering an
industry that many were actively seeking to flee.

But I still had the dream that had driven me since I
was a young boy, and I had the faith that there was an
opportunity to succeed against the odds. I knew that there
were huge challenges in the farming industry, but I also
believed that there was massive untapped potential in the
rural economy. And above all, I had faith in the idea of the
countryside, something that has motivated me ever since
I was working in my father's allotment, dreaming of what
a proper green space would be. For me, it has always been
something of an ideal and as a result, I have never bought
into the pessimism that surrounds rural Britain, both from
those who live in it, and those who are outsiders and seek
to write off the countryside as a backward and forgotten
land. Not only do I love the countryside, but I think it
holds great potential: in a world where people are rushing
around in ever-busier cities, living ever-busier lives, there
is a great deal to be said for places where the pace of life
is more congenial, people actually talk to each other, and

you can see that food comes from somewhere beyond the supermarket shelf or the delivery van.

The business I have built has grown out of those values and those beliefs. It started with the support and loyalty of rural people, who sampled my products, recommended them to their friends and petitioned the supermarkets. And it has made its name through my unique position as a black farm owner in a mainly white part of the country.

None of that would have been possible without my own faith that I could break the mould, and my faith in the countryside as the basis for a winning brand. The evidence wasn't there to support my stupid idea. In fact the evidence was laughing in my face and telling me I was wrong. But I believed in it, and my experience shows that if you have faith in an idea and you base it on solid foundations, you can defy the critics and the smart-arses who think they know how something is going to turn out before you have even tried.

The evidence is only ever going to show you what is happening now. It can't completely tell you about what is changing, new trends and tastes that are emerging, and new opportunities to change the status quo. The best businesses are those that ride such waves of change, and that is something you cannot do without faith. Not a blind faith that good things will happen, but an informed faith in the possibility of change, and your ability to harness it. And if you spot the change that is about to happen, or have the means to make it so, then no one can stop you from achieving that dream. Your faith in the future is every bit as powerful as others' reliance on the present.

Finding believers

No religion has ever prospered without followers, people who show faith and find meaning in their belief systems. A business is essentially no different: to succeed you must build a tribe of believers, from your employees through to your customers, investors, advocates and even just the interested parties that follow from a distance. The idea that started in your head will soon have to travel much further than you can ever propel it yourself. If you are to succeed, you need an army of people who will be doing the hard work of promotion and recommendation.

It's the most basic rule of marketing, one I spent years telling clients about when I ran my agency. It is far better to have others talk well of you, than it is to do the talking yourself. The real work of any brand is to get the right people talking about you. Word of mouth is the most precious, most elusive asset for any business. A customer who has faith in your business is a hundred times more valuable as an advocate than someone with a clear vested interest.

That is the case because people don't really believe what advertising tells them. A good advert will catch the eye and intrigue someone, win their consideration and perhaps get them to do their own research. But it doesn't win the argument on its own. What does convince people is what their friends think, and what trusted sources tell them. It's why we scour Amazon reviews before we buy products online, and why we probably won't try a new restaurant or stay in a hotel without checking what others say about it on Yelp or TripAdvisor.

We have become obsessed about what other people think. The Internet has opened a portal onto a world of opinions, reviews and comparisons – scrutiny such as brands have never been subjected to before. All of this makes it more important than ever that a business has a willing tribe of people who are spreading the word of your good deeds. You need to get people believing in you, and to do that you need some disciples and apostles all of your own.

That has always been the ethos behind The Black Farmer. Before we ever got close to a supermarket shelf, we were touting our wares around farm and country shows, letting people try the sausages and see this curiosity for themselves. We were also one of the first brands to start featuring the logos of the main social media platforms on our packaging; today that is the norm, but we cottoned on early to the power of a social network. We have always looked for ways to engage that network, to make a connection and give some ownership over our brand to the people who buy it and talk about it online. That has involved getting people to vote over new flavours and packaging: after all, if you aren't going to let the people these products are for have a say, what is the point? We have also done special editions featuring some of the faces of the large number of customers who submitted their pictures to take part. We are living at a time when people want to be more than just passive consumers. They want to share their opinion, talk about the things they love and hate, and have their voices heard. The best brands provide a platform for those conversations to take place, and they listen to what customers are telling them, as much as your local butcher, baker and grocer do in small towns like where I live. Social media is a forum to build those relationships on an industrial level; a means of finding the people who will show and spread faith in your business.

Having a network of such supporters must be the aim of any brand in today's market. Yet before you can build a big tribe, you need to start a small one. And before there can be customers, there must be the people who will help you get to market. For a lot of entrepreneurs, the most difficult conversation is the first one you have with someone you need to convince to back you. That could be your first hire, your first investor or an essential partner whose support you need to enlist. As I said, I drew a blank when trying to get unsecured finance from the banks. But, while that was something I could get around, the one thing I could not live without was a manufacturer, and it was a local producer, Steve Turton at Westaways, that agreed to work with me. He had no need or obligation to work with me, but he saw the opportunity and had the courage to back us when we were nothing. Without their support, and their faith in the idea of creating something exciting and new on the market, we could never have got going in the first place.

You will find yourself having many such conversations, selling yourself and your idea to people whose backing you need. And that is where the religious analogy is relevant again, for you are really the prophet and preacher for your brand, the lone voice who is pushing this idea forward and trying to convert others to the same belief. And just as religions have learned down the centuries, there are some who will come and join you, while others remain stubbornly agnostic. Believers lapse and need to have their faith restored, and there are always those yet to be reached and open to being converted. It is never easy. And you need the energy, the commitment and the fervour of the preacher if you are going to get others to show the same faith in you as you have in yourself.

Faith to carry on

The thing about faith is that it is not a constant. It is not something you can switch off and on, but a deeply emotional part of you that must be looked after and renewed on a regular basis. When it comes to religion, there are some people who lose their faith, renouncing the beliefs they used to hold and everything associated with them. Suddenly, what had seemed certain contains only doubts and questions.

When you are pursuing a big dream, there are going to be moments when you have your faith challenged. That could be the faith you have in yourself, when you make a mistake or error of judgement. It could be the faith in your idea that is shaken when it doesn't get the reception that you had hoped or expected. Others you depend upon can lose their faith in you at a crucial point. You should take it as read that you will experience some combination of all three, at different moments in your journey. It is a fundamental part of a life lived with jeopardy, which requires you to continuously get better and adapt to ever-changing circumstances. A person who never wavers in their belief is probably not thinking enough about the challenges that lie ahead of them. There is such a thing as being too confident.

When you find your faith undermined, there isn't always a reassuring answer to the question of what happens next. You can't be sure there will be another client, a different supplier or a better offer. When you lose an important piece of the fragile jigsaw that is your company, it's hard to just carry on without a certain sense of trepidation. You start to think about the consequences, and to doubt what the way forward looks like.

When we were still running Commsplus we lost, out of the blue, our biggest client, Raymond Blanc. We'd been doing what we thought was a very good job, but someone else persuaded him to switch agencies, leaving us high and dry. One moment things are fine, you've got everything under control, but then something big like that falls away and you feel the dark clouds rolling over you. All those commitments that are forever at the back of your mind – paying the mortgage, making payroll – come rushing to the forefront. You feel the desperation start to creep up on you.

If I remember rightly, that night I did offer up a silent prayer. And the next morning, like any other, I had to get out of bed, go to work, pick up the phone and get on with the day's work. That is the faith you need to have when you feel the waters closing over you. Not a blind faith that everything is going to be OK regardless. But a sense of resolve that, if you keep on doing the right things and putting yourself about, the bad luck won't last forever. In that case it did not; another important client, one that had not been in our sights, proved to be just around the corner. Luck, faith or good business? You decide.

It's so important to remember that you cannot control everything in life. There are a great many things you can influence, but there is a limit to any individual and any team's ability to make things happen. Sometimes, whatever the rights and wrongs, and despite your best efforts, people will decide against you and there is nothing you will be able to do about it. When that happens, the key is not to let a jolt to your inner belief become a crisis of faith, in which you start to question everything and get stuck on the problem. The moment of greatest danger is when you start committing your energies to examining the past, rather than facing forwards. If you allow yourself to wallow in misery for even a short time, then you risk everything, because you have taken your eye off the ball and are not doing the things you must to recover from the setback. You need to get over your disappointment and sense of injustice, put it to one side and keep on going. You might even have a routine or ritual that helps you to do this. Mine was a piece of music, 'I'm Going All the Way' by Sounds of Blackness. That was what I would put on when something had gone wrong with one of my businesses, and I wasn't immediately sure where to turn. It is a mantra that reminds me of the promise I made to myself as a young man, and that having come this far I'm not going to give up now. We will all face these moments of crisis and doubt, and it is by restoring faith in ourselves and our work that we can overcome them.

In recent years, undoubtedly the greatest crisis I suffered was the leukaemia that took me to the threshold of death's door. That is when I learned anew the power of this agnostic faith to carry you through the things you cannot control. After my diagnosis, I realised there were two ways I could respond: like some people do, I might seek to micromanage the disease, going through all sorts of changes in my life to try and fight it, with extreme diets and whatever else people do when they are panicking and searching for some hope to grab hold of. Or I could accept that the only possible control I had over this disease was my attitude towards it, and my faith that – if it was meant to be – that some higher power would help see me through. And through whatever combination of luck, science and fortitude decides these things, I pulled through.

We do not really understand what makes the difference at this margin between life and death after science and medicine have done their best, but the outcome is still perilously balanced. This is why people who disregard faith as mumbo jumbo and superstition are, in my view, badly mistaken. They seek an objective, logical explanation for everything, when there are so many things in the world that we still do not understand. Whether or not you are religious, there is a place for faith to fill the gaps that logic, reason and science cannot. When you are embracing jeopardy, you will encounter many situations that are unfamiliar, challenges that seem unreasonably daunting and questions you do not fully understand. You are venturing into a world where what you know is dwarfed by the things you do not. And you need that essential faith – in yourself, in your ideas and from other people – to answer the questions you cannot and to carry you through.

CHAPTER 11

Count on hope

Throughout this book I have talked about the different things you will need to live a life with jeopardy, and how to deal with both the challenges and opportunities that will create. I now want to end by discussing the importance of hope, a small word that I actually believe is one of the most powerful in the English language. It is hope that is really the very basis for everything I have talked about here; as it has been the foundation of the things I have achieved in my life.

Hope is the place from which our dreams, passions, positive attitude and willingness to take risks arise. Hope is what helps get us past our fears and through adversity. And when the darkest hour comes, when you have lost everything else and have nothing left to defend you, hope is the last thing you have left with which to fight back. I know this because I have experienced what it feels like to finally lose hope. That was the worst moment of my illness, the period of a few days when I was convinced I was about to die. This was after the stem-cell transplant, the most radical treatment they can throw at you as a leukaemia patient. My doctors had got the disease under control, but told me it was not enough. Without going further, it was going to return and it was going to kill me. The only option, they told me, was to undergo a stem-cell transplant, something many people do not survive and which carried with it a list of warnings as long as your arm.

Until this point I had been relatively stoic about the treatment; I hadn't lost my hair, and it didn't feel as bad as people had warned me. So I was perhaps taking the warnings about this transplant with a pinch of salt. And then they did it, and the aftermath was worse than anything I had ever known. It was just awful; I stopped eating – in fact, everything seemed to stop. It got so bad that I thought even death must be better than this. For two or three days, I almost shut down, and I was really just lying there in the hospital bed, waiting to die. It wasn't a question of if, but when, because for the first time in my life I had given up.

Never before, not when I was growing up deprived, not when I was told I would never amount to anything, not when I was banging my head against a wall trying to get into the television world, not when I lost my most important client, had I ever lost hope. But in that moment, over those few days, my spirit was drained and I had nothing left to fight with.

The only explanation I can give for my recovery is that I got bored with waiting to die. I had resigned myself to death, but it did not come. And then slowly, agonisingly, things started to get a little better. The battery of hope was somehow recharged a little, just enough to make me see that there was a future ahead, to give me back my resolve and my will to fight. And slowly, painstakingly, I climbed my way out of that hole. It took time, because after a procedure like that nothing is normal again for a very long while. You face challenges every day as you inch towards key milestones: one hundred days without the transplant being rejected, one year and then two. All along the way, you are threatened by infections and complications that can wipe out your progress or even kill you.

I had always believed in hope, but I never knew its true power until the moment I lost it. Seeing how the loss of hope almost led me to death, and rediscovering just a sliver of it, helped me to fight my way back towards life. There must be very few words that can really hold the power over life or death, but I believe that hope is one of them. I know it is what saved me.

Hope is so important in our lives, because without it none of the other things I have talked about become possible. You cannot dream big dreams, you cannot let your passions rise, you cannot tackle fear, uncertainty and adversity unless you are coming from a place of hope. To embrace jeopardy and seize the opportunities that unlocks, you need to have a fundamental belief that a better tomorrow lies ahead, and that you yourself are capable of making it happen. This hope of a better life is what has motivated people to push for progress throughout human history. It is why my parents' generation left their homeland to come to a strange place that did not really want to accept them; because they had hope that it offered something better, if not for them, then for their children.

Hope is what has been behind every business that has ever been created; every political movement that has been started; every campaign for social progress that has been launched. The world becomes a better place because enough people have hope that it will, and that hope inspires the actions that are needed to make change possible. And that, when you are starting on this road to a life with lived jeopardy, is where you must begin; with the fundamental sense of hope that you can achieve something better, live the life you want, and look forwards, upwards towards your dreams. For without hope, what is the point of even trying?

Hope for change

Any dream you might have, anything you want to achieve, starts from the same place: a hope that things can be better. It might be about a better life for ourselves and our family, a better life for other people or a better way of doing things that people have always done the same way. Everything I have done in life ultimately came from the hope that I could live a better life than my parents, in a better place than the inner city where I was growing up. It was that hope that helped create the dream to own a farm, the ambition to work in television and the desire to start working for myself. If I had not had that hope, I would have fallen at every hurdle that I encountered on that journey. And if I had not rediscovered hope at my lowest ebb, I am certain that the complications of my stem-cell transplant would have killed me.

Hope provides the spark that dreams are built on.

Perennial pessimists do not build great businesses, they do not explore new opportunities and they do not burn with the desire to change things. The survivor's mentality I have talked about is fundamentally one in which you are living without serious hope in your life. You might have hope for a nice dinner at the end of the day, or that your team is going to win at the weekend, but no real hope for a better life, for something more fulfilling and for an escape from the things that drag you down.

By contrast, people who are willing to embrace jeopardy are living with hope, powered by the belief that a better future is possible. That hope is what allows them to tackle the challenges of the unknown, and to take the risks necessary to pursue big dreams. Without hope in the future, you are going to remain forever stuck on the starting line, stuck in the life that you wanted to change.

Hope for change is one of the most powerful ideas in our culture. It is the foundation of many of the greatest political campaigns we have witnessed. Remember the red and blue posters from Barack Obama's 2008 election campaign? They only needed a single word to sum up the promise of Obama as a candidate, his commitment to change the United States and build a better future. And of course that word was hope. The idea of hope summed up all the emotions and expectations that were vested in the USA's first black President; for once it is probably no exaggeration to say that the entire world was watching as he swept to victory. It was the hope he inspired that motivated voters to turn out in record numbers to elect him.

It was during that election campaign that some of

Obama's opponents sought to use the idea of hope against him. The former New York Mayor, Rudi Giuliani, said in a speech that 'Change is not a destination, just as hope is not a strategy.' And with regard to the intricacies of government, he may have been right. Not all of the hope created by the Obama campaign was fulfilled when he reached the White House. But when it comes to people's lives, Giuliani could not have been more wrong.

We will never be able to calculate how many people – in the USA and around the world – were inspired by Obama's example and the hope he gave people. It might not have been enough to push through every bit of legislation he wanted, but it had a huge impact beyond the corridors of power. And in the lives of individuals, hope and change are two of the most important things we can hold onto and believe in. For to achieve the things we want in life, we are all going to have to change: change our circumstances, change the way we act and learn new things along the way. None of that is possible unless you are beginning from a place of hope. When you are just starting out on the road to change, the hope in something better may be one of the only tools you have. You must grasp it, for it is also one of the most important.

Hope for better

I believe hope is so important to our lives because it is really where our emotions exist at their most fundamental. We have hope for the future, hope that there is goodness in our fellow human beings, and hope that we will be able to overcome the worst that life can throw at us. New things – whether it is relationships beginning, children being born or new ventures being undertaken – are at their core an expression of our hope for something better. The things we care about most and invest our greatest emotional energies in are all about finding new ways to have hope.

Hope is not only something that allows us to embrace jeopardy in our lives; it is also a necessary part of the tool kit for overcoming the challenges that creates. When you let in jeopardy, you are essentially agreeing to give up on the idea of certainty to chase the hope of something better. You may put aside someone else's pay cheque in favour of working for yourself. You give up trying to live up to someone else's expectations and instead start pursuing your own dream. Above all, you accept that what some people call stability is actually an illusion, and that only by chasing jeopardy can we achieve the things we want.

I believe that jeopardy is necessary for a better life, but that does not mean I am pretending it is easy. Taking on new challenges means encountering new hurdles, having to develop new skills and growing a thick skin. That is where hope plays its part again: not just in helping you begin the journey to a better life, but in equipping you to survive it. You are raising your life's level of difficulty, because by doing so the rewards of success are that much greater. And you are surrendering any pretence you ever had to certainty about what is going to come tomorrow, and how you are going to deal with it.

It is only with hope – and only with the faith in yourself and your ideas that we discussed in the last chapter – that you can navigate the obstacle course you are choosing to undertake. Hope fills the gaps between what we know and what we are yet to discover. It keeps us going when the next bend in the road ahead isn't yet visible through the fog. And it gives us the strength to fight back against the worst setbacks we will experience.

When I got ill, I didn't know whether or not I was going to survive. There was no certainty about whether the treatments would work, whether I would escape the maze of possible complications or if my body was strong enough to survive the attack it was under. Like every cancer patient, I had to go through the terror of losing control over my future, outsourcing it to the brilliant doctors and nurses of University College Hospital. The only thing I had left was my hope that I could overcome the situation I found myself in, and my hopes for what I still wanted to achieve in life should I get better. A simple attitude that was about saying whatever the circumstances, I shall not yield. And it was only when I briefly lost that hope, in the despair of the condition the transplant left me in, that I seriously contemplated the thought of death.

If you are going to take the advice of this book and accept jeopardy into your life, then that will bring many challenges, as well as opportunities in its wake. I do not want to sugar-coat the reality for you. It is as hard as it can be rewarding. Dreams do not happen easily for a reason. But if you can find and nurture hope, that fundamental belief in the possibility of a better tomorrow, then you can fight any and all of the difficulties you will face. And it is only when you no longer have any hope of success, only when the last scrap of inner belief has been snuffed out that you should consider giving up on your dream.

Hope for tomorrow

As I have got older, and started to achieve the things I first dreamed about as a boy, the things I hope for have changed with me. When you are young, you are necessarily quite focused on yourself and the things you want to achieve. I was no different: it was all about my life, the low expectations people had of me, and what I myself could do to overcome them.

With age, and with some of those ambitions achieved, comes a different perspective. When you are married, have children of your own and have started to achieve what you first set out to do, your focus starts to shift to other people. You no longer have to be so selfish, and can think of the power you now have to help others. The greatest thing in life is being able to give back; to help others achieve their dreams just as you once set out to do with the same passion.

Today, I focus as much on the hope I can inspire in other people as on hopes I still have for my own life and my family. In particular, just as I once strove to prove the point that a black man could be a rural landowner and a farmer, I now want to use the position I have to help improve the lives of others like me, particularly young black people who still face so many unfair challenges with attitudes ingrained in society and in industry that tip the balance against them. No one knows better than me, who grew up in an environment which was really devoid of hope in many ways, of the power of a positive example. You cling onto the people and stories that give some flicker of indication that a better life is possible. The things you see and hear that offer hope are like the oasis in a desert and you drink deeply from them.

As this book has shown, I have unashamedly made my name and my business as being the only black farmer in the UK, or at least one of the only ones. But if that moniker has been of huge benefit to me, it is not one I ever really hoped to keep. Instead, my great hope was, and is, that my example can provide some kind of inspiration to others. I want the next generation of young black people to see that there are possibilities for them beyond inner-city life, and that the countryside is a place of opportunity if they are willing to seek it out. In fact, it would be nothing short of a travesty if I am still one of so few black farmers in a decade or two's time.

There are so many preconceptions about whether black people are welcome in rural England and so many of them are false, coming from people who have never come near the place. The whole point of being so mouthy about being a black man owning a farm in the south-west has been to show what nonsense that really is. If I can do it, make a noise about it and make a success of it, then why not anyone else?

This isn't just an idle hope I have held onto. For several years I ran a Black Farmer scholarship scheme, bringing a dozen young black and Asian teenagers from the city to the countryside, giving them an experience of what it is like to work on a farm and to live a different sort of life. It wasn't easy for any of us, but I wanted to reach kids who had been as difficult and bloody-minded as I had been at that age. When the first dozen scholars arrived, however, they got exactly the welcome they had expected. Or to be exact, they were seeing racism everywhere, interpreting people's looks for what they were not. It was only when I got the teenagers to talk to the locals that they realised they were actually friendly, curious and cared about helping them.

The results were mixed: I had two girls walk out of the first scheme in protest at a punishment I had set of sleeping outside in tents and getting up to milk the cows at 3am. I told another boy, who just wanted to spend the whole time challenging my authority, that he had to leave too. But one of the graduates went on to study agriculture as one of the first black students at his college. Two more stayed on for a year to work for me at The Black Farmer. I certainly didn't begin my scheme expecting that all the kids were going to find their dream working in the rural economy. But I think we opened some young eyes to new opportunities, and helped them to realise that alien things and places are not always the way other people tell you they are going to be.

The experience also gave me an insight into the reality for young people growing up in the same inner cities as I had decades previously. What I quickly realised is that many of these guys had become experts in gaming the system they were familiar with, which meant manipulating the guilt complexes of city-dwelling white liberals. They were probing for points of weakness, things they could interpret and exploit as racism. I hate this victim culture because it is the opposite of what I think young people need to succeed in life. It actively corrodes the inner strength and self-belief that can get people on the path to self-sufficiency. It is almost as much of a handicap as the open bigotry that was once the norm. Well-intentioned people think they are helping with their guilt, but they are actually doing harm.

The guilt complex is everywhere you look. We saw it again recently when there was a Tory MP who was recorded using the phrase 'nigger in the woodpile'. The white liberal establishment predictably piled in on this poor woman, who I do not believe was guilty of anything except a clumsy choice of words. It would not have crossed her mind that what she was saying would be interpreted as racist. My view is that those who criticised her so readily, and called so confidently for her to step down, need to look at their own records, on diversity, hiring policy and support for young people from ethnic minorities. It is so easy to condemn others, but what are you yourself doing to make the situation better, except participating in the blame game whenever someone gets it wrong? Really, it all stank of hypocrisy and the desire of people to feel good about themselves at someone else's expense. Meanwhile, they would have had plenty of questions to answer were the spotlight shone on their own lives.

My hope is that we can get beyond the place we have reached with race in this country, where we readily acknowledge that not enough young people from ethnic minorities have sufficient opportunities to get on in life, but have few proper solutions to deal with the problem. There are a lot of warm words and good intentions to reassure people that something is being done, but in reality these are getting us nowhere. Instead, we need some radical action. For instance, in broadcasting, if diversity was one of the criteria for how programmes get commissioned, you would see change happen overnight. It can be done, but it would take the people who do well from the current system to make changes that would favour others.

The same shift is needed in my own industry, and I believe there could be no better sector than food to own the challenge of properly representing their customer base as it actually exists today. I know better than most what the reality is of being a black guy trying to make your way in the retail industry, dealing with people at management level. As I said to an employee I recently hired, who is black, you have to get used to all sorts of small indignities. Twice I have been mistaken for a minicab driver. Plenty of times I am referred to as coloured. And believe it or not, you will also be complimented on 'not being like a normal black person'.

The simple fact is that you will see many black and ethnic minority faces on the shop floor of the nation's supermarkets, but far fewer if you make it to the board-room. I recently contacted all of the UK's major food retailers and manufacturers to inquire about their diversity policies and representation of ethnic minorities at a senior level. It is clear, as the likes of Tesco, M&S, Sainsbury's and JLP told me, that there are diversity targets in place. The big retailers are not blind to this issue. I was less impressed by suppliers, with only five out of fifteen major groups I contacted even giving the courtesy of a reply.

These are companies that are on the frontline of the battle for a fairer society, in which people of all colours and creeds should have a fair opportunity to succeed. Everyone eats and we all buy food. Yet the people making the decisions about how we do that are still, despite the good intentions that undoubtedly exist, grossly unrepresentative of the people they sell to.

The challenge of true racial equality has to be about more than targets and ticking boxes, though I do not criticise any business for seeking to measure something that is so important. Over and above that, though, there also has to be a cultural recognition about the unconscious biases that exist, the invisible barriers in many people's way, and the tendency for people to hire in their own image. We have a long way to go.

But I have hope that change can be made to happen, one based on all the life experiences I have talked about in this book. Where too many black people currently feel there is no place for them – be that in the media, in agriculture or politics – I know that this does not have to be true. My whole life, I have taken myself into industries and environments where it was thought people of my race, and with my education, could not go. From television to farming, I have found that where you might expect there to be an unfriendly welcome, the opposite is often true. It was the same when I ran to be a Member of Parliament in the 2010 General Election. I was chosen as the Conservative candidate for Chippenham, a market town in Wiltshire, the epitome of Middle England. Now the stereotypical view would have been that the pension-age local members might have been a little doubtful, to say the least, about me. The truth was far from that: not only did those people have the courage to choose me, a political outsider, as their candidate, but they could not have campaigned harder to try and get me elected in what turned out to be a very close-run ballot. Those women, and they tended to be women, in their sixties and seventies would merrily tramp around in the rain, knocking on doors, introducing me to voters and doing everything in their power to win the vote.

What my experiences have taught me is that stereotypes can be subverted, today's reality does not have to last forever and prior expectations can be disproved by actual experiences. By venturing into unknown territory, I have proved to myself time and time again that the only truly closed doors in life exist in our minds. And if we can open those, and carry real hope that things will get better, then we can achieve almost anything we set our minds to. That is the attitude I still have in my life and that is the message I would like people to take from this book. Change is hard but it is not impossible, whether in individual lives or across society as a whole. What people are dreaming of today can be made to happen in the future. Achieving that is something that is fraught with jeopardy, but only by embracing such jeopardy – by harnessing the power of hope – that the better future we are all striving for can be realised.

As you finish this book and start to think about how you can embrace jeopardy in your own life, remember this. Before you can create change in your life, and start to achieve the things you want, you need to believe that something better is possible. Before you can have a dream, before you can show the right attitude, before you can overcome adversity and take risks, you need to have hope. Don't start by thinking about the things you can't do; begin with the hope for what you could do. Let hope be the foundation stone for your dreams, and everything that follows. Some people will scoff at you, so let them. That ridicule is nothing more than the battle cry of the survivor, someone who doesn't have the courage to try something themselves, and doesn't want anyone else to have a go either.

As you begin your journey, to whatever destination you have chosen, you have something incredibly precious: the innocent, uncorrupted hope of what the future may bring. There will be time later to judge and critique your ambitions, to subject them to the harsh tests of logic and reason, and sort the serious dreams from the false hopes. But before all that, it is just you, your partners in work or personal life, and the things you hope to achieve. And that is as good a place to start as any I know.

The time is now

If you have made it this far, then I hope you are with me on the importance of jeopardy, and already starting to think of ways to embrace it in your life and career. As you ponder that, I would like to leave you with one final thought. And it is a simple one: get on with it! If you want to make a change, then make a start immediately. Do at least some things which move you towards the end goal, even if they are only small steps. The enemy of progress is procrastination, and if you put off what can be done today to tomorrow or next week, I can almost guarantee you will never get round to it at all.

Don't be one of those people who waits around, hoping that good things are going to happen; that a great job is going to fall into your lap; that you will somehow by magic meet the person you are meant to be with; or that the business idea in your head is going to grow legs and arms and build itself.

Don't let yourself be someone who lives with regrets, where you know you could have done and said things, but stayed silent and inactive, and let others take what could have been your place. Don't let your fear of what might go wrong prevent you from having a go at the things that matter most to you.

There is this terrible feeling in life and it can be summed up by two words: 'if only'. If only I had been brave enough, if only I had been able to make a decision, if only I had believed in myself. If only is a feeling worse than physical pain itself. Because you know it has nothing to do with any other person or external circumstance. It is not a wrong someone else has done to you, or an affliction that has been randomly visited upon you. It is something you have done to yourself; the only person responsible is you. You simply cannot have a life lived with too many 'if only' moments; it colours your view of the world and it shapes your very being as a person.

I can say this as someone now in his sixties, who has recently survived a serious illness, because I know that life is much shorter than we think it is going to be. When we are young we feel invulnerable and think that our lives will be as long as we want them to be. We think that there is all the time in the world. But as older readers will agree, life happens more quickly than we ever think possible. Time speeds up, things happen that absorb our energy and attention, opportunities emerge and pass us by. There is a world of possibility surrounding you, but only you can make something of it. It doesn't matter if you aren't in your twenties or just starting out on your career. It is never too late to make a change in your life, big or small, and to start working towards a dream you have always held, whether in the forefront of your mind or lodged somewhere towards the back, half-forgotten.

All the advice I have given in this book fundamentally relies on your willingness to go out and seek opportunities, to be someone who is outward looking, and always moving forward however difficult the circumstances. If there is an essential, shared mindset of people who live with jeopardy, it is proactivity. These people ask the difficult questions, they challenge themselves and others around them, and they have no shame in putting themselves forward to take on new responsibilities or to pursue fresh opportunities.

I say they, but it can just as well be you. You need to believe in yourself, rather than becoming one of those people who talks themselves down and rules themselves out. Learn to value the talents you have and ignore people who try and tell you what you can and cannot do. Be someone who takes a step forward, even if you are afraid to do so, feeling unsure of how others may react and lacking full confidence in your ability to deliver. Unless you take that first step, you are never going to take the many more that will be needed to achieve your dreams in life. No one can take away from you the things I have talked about in this book: your dreams, your passions, your faith and your hope in tomorrow. But at the same time, no one else can take that first step on your behalf. The desire and the determination to do so can only come from within.

Of course, it is all much easier said than done. There is jeopardy in everything I am trying to encourage you do to. But hopefully I have convinced you by now that this is actually a very good thing; that what you are initially afraid of can actually be a wonderful force for change and self-improvement. It is only through the embrace of jeopardy, the recognition that it is beneficial to push ourselves and experience uncertainty, that we can fulfil our true potential.

That in turn requires the acceptance that failure and loss are not the worst fates that can befall us as people. For me, the worst fate is to be someone who is left wishing they had done things differently, said what they thought more often, and risked more to go further. Regret is a terrible thing and it can be avoided, if you steel yourself to the demands of jeopardy, and throw yourself into a life where uncertainty is the norm. A life where you are constantly trying to stave off loss and failure is one where fulfilment drifts ever further away from you. You must banish this negativity and look forward, towards a better future and how you can achieve it.

Allow yourself to live for a while in a place of hopes and dreams, before you let the harsh realities of life crowd in and chip away. Push your ambition to its full height before you start to moderate and minimise it. Free yourself from self-imposed restrictions about what you want to do, what you are good enough to do and what your personal circumstances allow you to do. Allow yourself to take that first step into the jeopardy of the unknown, and see how it feels. Start there, and see where it takes you. And make sure you do it today.

Acknowledgements

I would like to thank Josh Davis for his help in writing this book and being true to my authentic voice. I was able to find my authentic self with the help of The Hoffman Process UK.

A very special heartfelt thanks to all my guardian angels. You all have helped me on my journey to success. This book is a testament to your love, kindness, support and belief. Without all of you watching over me, success would have stayed out of reach.

Thank you also to my agent Adam Gauntlett at Peters Fraser & Dunlop, and my publishers Anna Steadman and Zoe Bohm at Little, Brown for believing in this book and giving me an opportunity to tell my story.

Finally, I would like to thank you, the reader, for reading this book and I hope it inspires you on your journey to business success and personal development.

Index